Contents

Vol 95   No 1   Spring   2005

Poems

Essays

Reviews

Poet in the Gallery

Art

Poems

Stephen Knight

99 POEMS

i. m.

A face that, though in shadow, still appears
A graceful Child, his father's joy!
A ship-wrack on his bed, night being past
Abandoned by day in a pinkish lounge, his final
ahv naebawdy
'Allas!' quaþ he, 'now me is wo
Almost as true as his kindness, I'll say, almost as true as his laughter, his
                                         labored jokes

Ane faiding flour, away as wind it weiris
Angled to face each other
Are you to leave like this

Before you say
Below this faultless Stone, is laid
Bid mountain-light attend your bower
Brimmer Street irregular! Father's barbarous dress-sword

Carriages, clergymen, unsmiling faces, delicate hands
Cold rivers, colder seas, alas

Death's oompah band

'E weren't no bloomin' 'ero, all 'e did was live an' die
Empire State patrician

Fare-thee-well, o glaikit man
Farewel, more lov'd than any I recal
Father! how soon this night o'er-brims the trees
Fog after dusk, murmuring small requests
Fold the sky in half, shake out the stars
For he is affraid
fus ting dat crazy clack

Go, finde a Store of Tears among the Clouds
God of all things, all things rain and air, all flying things

He gave his Checks – the Whistle blew
He Rambld Ere The Mornings Dews Could Flee
He visited the loft, not long before
He was withouten any peere
He woke again last night, and cried
Here he sat, his face o'ershadowed
Here rests a gentle Man, whose modest Heart
Here shall be rest for evermo
His dreaming eyes, his brow in touch
His hat still on its peg. His shoes lined up
His watch-face like a skating rink
How still the moon-blanch'd sea
'How's the Humber? How's the wife? Do you remember Lilian?'

I dreamed you stood alone, in No Man's Land
I have seen Him in a meagre light
I sought, ô grassie mountaines, thy constant fellowship
I THOUGHT of Thee, unfathomable one
I took no part
Icy nim-air, a barn done Dinner Street
If Death, growne wearie of his warres
Il laisse tomber son modelling knife, *tant pis, tant pis*

Lately, I have seen the fellow with his pockets inside out
Lethean foam-flowers rise from the sewers
Like as a winde that fadeth ere blacke night
Lost in the pea-drills behind our house
LOVE NAILS   TriBeCa Nails   (too much

May his comfy shoes, O Lord
Mr Chips, Bulk Catering
My dreams of thee! How soon the morning comes!
My father had heard tell
My father picked up a stone
My latest thoughts return to thee

[. . .] nis þer no niȝte
Niver say tha'rt frit o' me
No murmur stirs your room, tonight, no voices call below
No nothin kin explain it, yes indeedy
No winde there blew, the skie was bare of anie bird

O thou whose falt'ring hand the waters tune
O turn thy Waters through my Heart
Oh, sweet was the rain as it fell on Swiss Cottage
Once my Lamentation was an envied horror

Plip plop plip

Sisyphus, your heart
Snow in the branches, where birds perch still as graves
Stars observe, with their flat blank eyes
Sythen in that spote hit fro me sprange

That was a crappy bookstore smell, *jeez.* Old guys
The fields of snow did breathe
The laundromat is crowded. Every ghost
The sea it was brazen and icy
The Show'r come down on Tory and Whig, Dust gone to Mud
The stairs became more difficult
Thy Exile from this World, deare Friend
Thy Publick Virtue, Father, all attest
'Tis three years since, his grave is bare

Uh-oh

Vnmesurable greiff, Alas! how straunge is this
Voices on the wireless

We are becoming
Weepe with me, to night, all hope is over-come
Well, then! Let no man disapprove
When first your slender breath
When the evenèn wind do blow vrom zight
Where rootless poppies lie
Who could not stay a while

Yf all my wordes were raine upon thy grave
Yonder
You could not face me, then
You could not speak, nor even smile, before you turned
You cupped one hand to catch the crumbs
Your hands

Claire Lockwood

IN COLD BLOOD AND THUNDER

Late afternoon comes to weight
like a grouper or some other
deep-sea feeder. It holds
your breath in this languorous stretch
that builds to the rolling break
of the heart
beating the last
days' wait away

Still it swells but still
it will not rain.
Instead it stirs the bed,
shifting the springs
so each itch each judder
is steeled to remain
singing in unseen spirallings
rocking you softly like long slow hours of A and E
at that time in the night when the light sits
on green. The low-loaders bolster
the hard shoulder. Bellies almost
out. Or back doors open. No No
nothing to be stolen as tender as golden
as this day as pressing as the rest
effortless on
                your sleeping breath

STEM

hell yes, done to death, but
ideally the cut carnation should really
be displayed in a plain glass vase against
resounding white. So showing
the submerged bird-leg knots. Each
once a tentative sprouting out. Each
of these tiny climaxes! Each
never now the main event but each
a job of work been done, each
a soft spot overcome, each
a skirmish fought and
like the swan,
their bunched heads preside
imperviously on.
Here is no head
for those hard sums,
nor heart for the limp
damp fact all told
in sinuous form or scattergun.
It is but to taste red
and red again against
the rain of today
and its godawful dribbing
and drab.

SONG

            what
you had in the
years, in the
years spent in
patting, in
patting your
belly and
rubbing your
head

            what
you had in the
bag, in the
strength of
the bag still
holding, holds
all in, holds
your chattels
home

            what
you had in the
asking (you
had to go
asking) you
had in the
wanting of
the bitter
passed

          what
you had in the
scaffolding,
in weights and
in pulleys,
you had you,
you fool you,
placed in my
driving

          what
you had in the
sewing, so sewn
in the notes in
the cuffs and
the collars
of persons
unknown

          what
you had in the
nights in, the
nights sat
in stitching,
in *kind words*
are hanging
about your
neck

          what
you had in the
waking, the
waking and
stretching, the
waking and
rubbing your
eyes, had been
missing

          what
you had in the
waking, the
waking and
gazing, dazed
and adored:
a small blond
boy in a bear
house

Mimi Khalvati

GHAZAL

after Hafez

However large earth's garden, mine's enough.
Love's rose and the shade of a vine's enough.

I don't want more wealth, I don't need more lies.
In the dregs of a glass, truth shines enough.

What else can Paradise offer beggars
and fools? What ecstasy, when wine's enough?

Come and sit by the stream. Rivers run dry
but to carry their song, a chine's enough.

Balance the books, read the sorry account.
Any book with a broken spine's enough.

When you're here, my love, what more could I want?
Just mentioning love in a line's enough.

Heaven can wait. Since you opened your gates,
no heaven however divine's enough.

I've no grounds for complaint. As Hafez says,
isn't a ghazal that he signs enough?

John Ashbery

TENSION IN THE ROCKS

They changed for dinner. In those days
no one was in a hurry, it was real time
every time. Usually the streets were saddled with fog
at night. In the daytime it mostly blew away.
We kept on living because we knew how.
Mapleseeds like paperclips skittered in the *allées*.
We knew not how many enthusiasts climbed the slope,
nor how long they took. It was, in the words of one,
"beholding" not to know. We eased by.

You can see how the past has come to pass
in the ferns and sweepings of ore and text
that shadowed such narratives as had been scratched,
as though any hotel guest could wipe the blight away
and in so doing, be redeemed for the moment.
I tell you it was not unseemly.
Little girls gathered in groves to see the wish spelt out,
yet under the hemlocks all was moulting, a fury
of notations, obliterated. We knew who to thank
for the postcard. It was signed, "Love, Harold and Olive."

HEAVY HOME

. . . hungry eaters of a slender substance – C. M. Doughty

One thing follows another awning in the event horizon. One life in the going changes the subject. Some things made sense, others didn't. I didn't expect to die so soon. Well, I guess I'll have to have tabulated myself in some way. I'd discussed writing on your leg. Others in the tree school groaned, stirred in their sleep, having lately put away childish things. All of us late. What if we lived overseas? We could survive on alms and pledges for a while, find jobs in the barrel industry, decoct melismas on which to build an echo.

Here we break camp; it was decreed by an elder, or alder. He put the water on to boil. He sends us itches and the wherewithal to scratch them, fossils in the guise of party favors. Then sprang dull-headed into the gilded surround, chimera after all. Tears from the doll leaked out. It was as if we had chosen this path on a different journey, and were waiting in the deafening wilderness for our instincts to catch up, leggy hope.

Many flushings of the toilet later you'll give it back and we'll give it to the mechanical oracle, render unto caesura, and expect thrifty thanks, somewhere between laughter and obloquy. But how quaint the semicircular drive and its trimmings: gazing globe, lark's mirror, lime twigs, tinsel, ormolu, Venus's fly trap, *pattes de velours*, Rembrandt and his goat. On a return visit we were not received, the grace period having expired.

The pictograph is also a chimera. Since day one you've abused it. Resting on our oars we breathe in the attar of dissent, breaking off of negotiations, recall of ambassadors, the rift within the lute. For the time being the disputed enclave is yours. But its cadence is elsewhere.

Andrew McNeillie

from GLYN DŴR SONNETS

(iii)

'Mr De Valera's Hint to the English in Wales'

'It is possible . . .' De Valera said,
addressing a thousand teachers at Caenarfon,
in nineteen-fifty, not urging a re-run
with fireworks at the Post Office and dead
in the streets come Easter to Caerdydd,
but out from Dublin simply to explain . . .
'. . . to lose your freedom and win it back again.
But lose your language and *Cymru am byth*
can never be but Wales forever lost.'
(I interpret the gist.) Ireland looked to
the Welsh example. Ireland knew the cost.
English should be taught as a second language.
And I'm thinking now I'd like to know
what the Home Office made of his homage.

(x)

When young Owain went to Bod Alaw,
the Welsh School in Colwyn (founded
in 1950), you'd think he was retarded,
and his parents thick. How could they allow
him to miss so much, fall behind forever,
in his rough flannel shorts, his pebble specs?
It made no sense. 'A language no one speaks,
except to the sheep and the weather.'

'Welsh-Welsh...' or 'thick Welsh,' they'd say meaning both
twp and spluttering guttural Babel.
As to their poetry! It beggars belief
that it doesn't translate, they'd sneer. As if
they knew all about the art of the *Awdl*
and *Englyn*, and the rules of *Cynghannedd*.

(ix)

A Monoglot Trout

First light, in England, travelling westward,
meets me looking for it, up for it at
scraich of innocence again, drop-of-a-hat:
a boy-man rising ten who clambered,
nervous at heart, to look time in the eye,
reticent in simple hope and silence
of loud wilderness: deliverance
that held me captive then, and will until I die.

When the bailiff came and said in English:
'I don't suppose you have a permit?'
Maredydd turned and offered him a fish.
I turned in silence and looked away.
So licence waived for a monoglot trout,
brithyll (in Welsh), we lived to fish another day.

(xii)

On the Study of Celtic Literature (1866)

for Robert Young, after Tom Paulin

'Didst not thou sow good seed in thy field?
From whence, then, hath it tares?' *Matthew* xiii, 27

'The sooner the Welsh language disappears,'
said St Matthew Arnold, '... the better'
and he meant every word to the letter.
Though he rattles on about wheat and tares,
as if in the name of sweetness and light,
make no mistake: what governs the page
of this *bien-pensant* Victorian Sage
is imperialist sweetness and shite.

Meanwhile, back at the Eisteddfod,
as high above the Irish Sea he stood
pontificating about the need to drive
the 'English wedge' into the very Welsh
-Welsh heart of Wales, the natives strove
to judge the best essay on: 'What it means to be English'.

(xiv)

'Mc maybe I am...' not aptly ap. Nor
did my father know Lloyd George, but he knew
Saunders Lewis; and others too who
had 'walked Fron-goch', with Collins, for
the duration of those Troubles we were spared
. . . except that time the IRA exploded
a bomb at Kinmel Army Camp in Clwyd
(so Brendan had thought to blow up Cammell-Laird)

. . . give or take a second home or two in Llŷn.
I'm no *Cymro*, no incendiarist either.
I live in middle England now, lost in
my middle years, found wanting too:
except that I know what I come from, and where,
bind me forever to my point of view.

(xvi)

The Irish Question

The time word takes to travel is unreal:
rumour's rampant, youths and rascals rally,
rabbles rouse, run ragged, rout, horrify:
next thing you know it's out of control.
Until . . . here's a party at a different game,
pursuing by stealth the English cause:
for Shakespeare's timely motive was
to put an Irish wolfhound in the frame.

For Owain read Tyrone. A fuse I lit
by chance in number three and fizzing in
fourteen explodes beneath my feet.
For Tyrone read . . . They stole from their own.
I pillage Henry for a line, just to begin
again, again . . . until all cover's blown.

Peter Gizzi

HOMER'S ANGER

i

Real things inside me he said.
You've gotten it all wrong.

I see you and hear you
and that is the beginning of a poem.

Not a circle but a ray
not a definition but a journey

flowering in scenes.
This composition is still all the time

coming into view.
The depth we might say.

I am seeing through you
like transistor songs

from a postcard beach town,
two loves caught in cinemascope.

A movement inside movement
unlike the stars and flag.

ii

I was going to tell you how it is
and then leaves out the window

ask me to respond.
Not just color and shine

but a total relinquishing
of the headlines.

If today is ash then
we have come from a great fire

and the heat is beginning
to consume the present.

To say rhythm is dangerous
is to miss the day entirely

to push the body on
in ungainly order

and the fate of fire
is to consume fuel from any source.

iii

Should we discuss the news?
The meteorological epiphenomena

day in day out. It's unforecastable,
not going to stop.

Here we are, caught
by a luminous blue fuzz

touching everything out our windows.
It's not what you thought.

The smell of earth and hot sun.
Reassuring to lilacs too.

Loneliness is structural after all,
you have to really come with us

across the page, and if we are
indeed, alone together,

mighty are the numbers
drifting out there.

iv

That's it then, everything opening,
memory fuzzing, dandelion projection –

a falling upward at last. If you can
move like those motes

casting random shadow casting
liberty, the low progress in air.

To Carthage I came, to shadow
the lovely outside pouring upon the desk.

The lowing flickering branch
making a picture to show you.

I searched, traveled in stacks
all day and now I've found you.

Empty light forming a dais
on the page. A valuable blank.

This craving for notes, momentum,
that I came to love the struggle,

inner engine spitting years,
splintered, what are years?

v

I am listening to a life
unlived any other way.

Think of it. The notes remain
even as the song-sparrows change

from dirt to egg. Spring
to spring. Maybe that's it.

The molecular world
falling and rising

within a single melody.
So why not liberty.

This is what I am told
to never stay with history.

Today we'll be talking
about the government.

It's important to remember.
All those scattered dispatches

on the back page. Human damage.
Working people and the right

to life, their pursuits,
not happiness,

not victories –
an endless series of victory.

vi

One eye is more green than another
one more gray, a golden band

circles both pupils, dilates
as the creature breathes.

One eye is best looking for police,
they circle the block.

One for waves and motion
undulating from trees.

The eye is an instrument of emotion
like memory lives in the mouth.

Do you know what I mean
when I say anger is not emotion

when everyone is stolen
I will begin in rain

not to be wrong
but uncertain, to want

more than this sentence.
If I say darkness is still

when it falls, understand
I am moving toward you.

Fiona Wilson

SOUR AUBADE

And did I curse you, as the sun got started
with its usual, smarmy hints, pink kisses
on strip malls and dealerships, the standard
business of sunbeams on the trees, trees, trees?

And did I weep, as first light showed up,
bad penny, relentless in the present tense
and I discerned a blue jay's sudden dip
to flight and the world became apparent?

My, my, my. How I loved the vague
expense of night, the window giving onto . . .
utter nothing . . . no narrative or ache
of detail, no haranguing to come to.

Now reflected in glass, I saw your grin
shining. Clear as day, my own poor bargain.

CELEBRITY

Perhaps it was a day like this – tired trees,
mizzle in twenty different shades of grey,
and mist, nothing if not general –that she,
a right wonder, sashayed in on the tide,
"a genius," as bold and sonsy as you please.

And perhaps it really was about "wit."
And perhaps her mouth truly was "sexy."
And perhaps she did insist on displaying
scars (she was down on the clamshell routine).
Perhaps. All this we may have seen and heard

as we lingered, average, on the quay,
eyes on her shape, the perfect oddity
of the outside-in so thrillingly near.
But what I recall is her puzzled stare
at us: "I thought there'd be more like me here."

SNUFF

I'm thinking we've taken a turn for the worse,
when the saturnine one, like the chancer he is,
sneakily slips his starboard hand,
just so, between her legs –
And, Jesus, the shadowy gallop now
as he bolts for the kill in the loch.

Julian Stannard

WHEN REFUSAL TO DO THE SHOPPING
MIGHT BE A CRIMINAL OFFENCE

The shopping list crackled on the kitchen table.
I said 'I can't possibly buy all of that.'
The woman who has shared my bed for fifteen years
crumpled the list into a little ball and shoved it down my neck.
'You *will* buy all of that', she said.
I removed the lump now burning into my neck
and dropped it onto the kitchen floor. 'I won't'.

The woman who's long rattled the edges of my defunct credit cards
said 'We'll see about that.'

I could hear her jabbing at the phone and chanting

one hundred and twelve
                                one hundred and twelve –

Then I listened to the outline of her case:
my English husband refuses to do the shopping
refuses to bring baskets of Mediterranean fruit to the marital table
refuses to drape cured ham over white plates
refuses to embellish the pasta with nut sauce
simply refuses, FUCKING R E F U S E S.
There was one long sob-filled silence.
Then yes, yes, yes I told you he was *inglese*.

I slumped into the sofa and listened to my life
breaking into awful, lovely pieces.
I started flicking through the TV channels
until I came across the Italian version of Who Wants To Be A Millionaire.
I changed my shirt and lit my wife's last cigarette.

Hours later there was a knock at the door.
I opened it and found a man in stylish uniform
holding two bulging supermarket bags from *dí per dí.*
his pistol clearly visible and his Puglian face lightly sweating.

When he'd put down the bags he saluted.

Every cherry pip you spat at me that night
made the scariest shape on the kitchen floor
and when you went in search of that baby sweet final cigarette
I casually mentioned the policeman had smoked it on his way out.

Fiona Sampson

PATH

Breathe

Trees deal
deal come up flickering deal flip-flap
leaves on a dark cheek.
                              Dark
grasps lighter dark

whereas a path
(you throw out a hand to scratch)
is making space out of itself space

opening its side:
                         wound which is not-tree

where the green breathing of trees
the lurch of space

Where your hand going about murders dark

the sleep of space.
Your hand
             refusing.

Where white is an hallucination

elder flowers are white gasps O O
opening like stings.
Everything drunk down to the ankles.

This is the not-taken
where we are
Trees flickering like candleflames
                                        the path
open-close of reluctance.

                        Breathe

                *

After-sleep space between the suddenly
mechanical eyelid and world:
after a weekend's drinking I feel the depression
like a solid thing.
                        Gestures,
turns to the left.

                Voices in the dark.

A child sleeping under the coverlet of voices.

All night, arguments in a train corridor, bang-rattle-
pop of the compartment latch
                                ne razumem. Explain

couplings hinges ratchets pivots busily

explain cables and bolts
scratch-scratching against skin.
Explain the length of a night-lit corridor vowelling vowelling.

The deep beauty is in fracture.

This is the way shank fits
to groove. This is the black oil

which is everywhere and not.

Za-zoooom. Under everything *the long retreating roar*
the long retreat under silky grey
under fields like groomed fur coming towards you
and away   Over, over and

spending

Explain says the child standing at the window,
her breath making morning fog.

＊

Blue-blond of headlights
making and unmaking darkness

                              like a jigsaw
(your hand under Grandma's)
on the hall table beside the rose bowl.

In that house
light here and there with its ruler

car engine closing its wings

while woodland moved
over the grass across the stream   moved

its thick fringe. Look

Up and
        up

look there
Tilt your head, it's all
in the angle of perception   This isn't the *a-b-c* classroom.

The child leans between gutters and gables   enunciating
the white world   annunciating *Look*

beyond the mown lawn the almost invisible
water searching about
          its narrow gutter

(hair ties bloom in grass):
        look
how it closes the space and draws shadows down over it.

ne razumem (Serbian) = I don't understand

Sinéad Morrissey

FLIGHT

There he saw one Anne Bridlestone *drove through the streets by an*
officer of the same corporation, holding a rope in his hand, the other end
fastened to an engine called the branks, which is like a crown, being of
iron with a great gag or tongue of iron; and that is the punishment which
magistrates do inflict upon chiding and scolding women; and he hath
often seen the like done to others.
– England's Grievance Discovered (1655)

After the murder of our blessèd Martyr,
After the slaughter of the rout at Worcester,
His son the rightful king went into hiding –
Here as a woodcutter, there as a serving-man –
Disguising the telltale milk-white of His skin
By the dye of rotted walnuts. 1651:
The Year of Our Lord that my husband bridled me
And I have learned to hold my tongue in company.

*

He could not remain unrecognised for long,
Majesty being so natural unto Him,
It soon shone forth. But was He loved!
He walked upon the bones of England,
Sought solace at farms and hid in the crowns of trees
And all of nature shadowed Him. His enemies
Sifted the land and still His face was not revealed.
It is my love of Him bleeds when I speak out loud.

*

He has stood in a fall of rain
While Cromwell's men sang psalms against Him
And did not venture in. He has seen women
Sink to their knees and then raise their hand in blessing.
My husband desires a sign.
But for all his reading of *Revelation*
I say heaven admits its own
And it is Him. The jaw-straps tighten.

*

The changeling Prince vanished to France.
Deadwinter dismembers us.
Christmas consumes its own bright fire
And blazes by its absence. There is too much law
To live by, and I have torn my face
In two by swallowing silence.
My husband leads me through the marketplace
As the village women gape.

Andrew Bailey

LODESTAR, POLESTAR

i.m. Peter Redgrove

Although he is now become lodestar, the water
that flooded the village I lived in was him
and still is him, for steeped in his substance
as I climbed the moonlit path from the water-village,
where the moonlight that lit the way was him,
my moondried self stayed redolent of him.

The north star sings: for you he is with me now.

Then I discipled myself to these uncommandments,
tried to find the stars in sunlit skylights, the doors
to dreams that do not leave or let you close them,
to other minds that fan and close like tarot decks;
I still endeavour, master, to be beesize, mothsize,
or so massive that the flesh that carries you can
seethe the dreams of mice from its pores to join
the tiny bestiaries choiring metamorphoses
among the grasses. The north star sings for me.

The stars that fall fall just as rain, and their ashes
dust clouds, making rain of him; the rain
makes plants of him, and so until we share him,
share his light, which holds still to that star
about which other stars, that are, as we are, him, rotate.

FROM THE CAVE PAINTING

Forgive the shoddy crafting – I have little time, here too the new have come,
their plates of clay, their tiny tools, their zeal to show us how. Too many
learn these marks that capture only sound, whose bison is two grunts,
two grunts, they will not feed on that. Remember where the language lies;

not in the words, but what they reach. Read this and recall;
will their sparrow-scratches bring rain, nurse crops from their husks,
bring fire from smoking hay? Will it last? It may be that language will sustain,
but I fear that we instead will pass, our hands the last to be language-stained.

If you read both language and their scritches do not read this; let the truth die
rather than be tamed to their spindling marks. If you believe, you can find us
in the cave in which the first mouth was first drawn, first drew breath.

Brian Henry

IN THE NEIGHBORHOOD OF HORSES

Daughter who tells me the hills are a moon

and you're jumping over it
not two inches off the ground,

a baby tucked beneath an arm
as the other guides you both up

and then higher until you're
where you say it's warmth,

I'd like to sit you down and talk
about the right way to orchestrate

a network of needs and desires,
to distinguish one from the other

before the lies you're allowed are forbidden
and your flight never leaves

the ground so hot below you,
the moon you will soon outstrip.

TO TODDLE

The tension you carry inside you
– so fragile no image could usher it –
produces what seems like a snapping
each hour, your body cycling
its fuel with such speed you are ever
sliding. Indentured to what
the body needs, you do not know
to pretend to be free from it.
Every action a link between *must*
and *must*. Your days, they will move
without you. Will move you
unawares. Speak for you.

Keston Sutherland

TORTURE LITE

Candied *faits divers* in frosted crackling, hurl myself
myself-mud immaterially scoffing up my fig
leaf face in a panto breakfast of hallucinations,
eating e.g. the "organ failure" niceties, August 1st
2002 *ex libris* U.S. Dept. of Justice, beneath it
all desire of oblivion runs out and is indifferently replenished,
or runs up another fine mess of print called nothing
worse than *a bill* or a reminder notice, iambic,
                                    —*then,*
smear that mud in an Oscars of libido-backed rash
tutting also to be eaten, or eaten for,
farcical parataxis on heat and / or low heat, taking care
suck off my hands, grace to get it under the
dumb eyelids and *commedia non scritta* in the stretching
cheek torn up about all this crying
                                    please no wait
                                    Il Dottore I: The Sex Mishap
                                    pillar of the human
                  arrangement II:
                                    pleased
                                    no / wait /
you that security is an indispensable pillar of
salt-lick you can make anyone say anything
the Blunkett-Clarke horse, a balaklava in your Yakult
spine cooler, *listen to this chatter—*

  - that men do not forfeit
  - who claim that we hate
  - if so,

the limit of honor in order to protect the freedom
Välkommen till Svensk Energi! *den is a country of*
endless possibilities. The classic defence is
the ticking bomb scenario: the ticking box scenario
comes *before* and *after.* Who do not sleep
under your oppression and diol. The squirrel ornament
is replaced: you remembered. And the helical
duck lays back and thinks open its polyurethane fundament
that makes foam guts spill on it and scratching a
noise but why, but fuck, all that. Pressing the gas with
her foot vanishes. They wrapped him in the flag
of Israel

                                    Spavento, Meo Squasquara
                                    XI: The Sex Is Right

            an arrangement

                            we can come

            to sure,

                            with strobe lights on

            for him MC:

                            out his hair / or not
sing Albert for all your life sing the dolphins fairly
mutter in their tank. Not without practising
I don't. And if Sergio were Michael Levin? But
he isn't in a bad state of permanent emergency.
You know when you were a kid you would smack
any person who pissed you off but you are now better off
and it is that special time of year. In the ear
soup some unthinking *fonctionnaire maudit* tips a shit
load of L'Oréal, the foreign insurgent snorts up
the shit-like incense of his own fanatical skin cooking,
Larkin in the air, the net curtains nailed down.

Lee Matthews

LEE'S BROKEN RED ECHO CHAMBER

Cooking as good a place as any;

Me at the stove: "where things begin might not suggest where they end
nor show what follows"
"Cumin is not a good indicator of a finished con carne" – part of another list.

Everything is just pieced together.

The red truck saying L E E was given to me when I was five-ish. It was a
wicked puzzle!
I always made sure that the letters would be last in.

On the train last week someone talked about Franz Marc, can you
believe it! But I had been to the Lechbaunhouse! My ears were burning!

– who hears *me* and can teach me and doesn't?

King Tubby trimmed the barber.
Leadbelly picked a bale of cotton.
Yokota sampled Murcof and made 'Lost Ring'.

At times everything is available.

Mostly. But imagine Jess' embaracement:
She walked across the frozen pond (after pawing at the ice for hours) and
leapt onto the water filter.
                    Or so she thought.

The lid was not on!   All streaky wet rat across the patio!
A few days later, as a gesture, she devoured a sparrow whole infront of me –
      even the legs and beak!

In some cities hawks are employed to keep pigeon numbers down
                    I like pigeon and also crows and seagulls.
My brother has a phobia of turkeys.

Both of us made a decision about what is valuable.

The life of birds! The mimic bird imitates chainsaws in the jungles of South
America!

Was that on tv?   Like the lichen?   Incredible.
          Motionless in the valleys of the Antarctic.

  There is that saying isn't there, about tragedy and man and man not being
able to stay in his own room?
                    But then again there is the saying that the tragedy of
life is not so much what we suffer but what we miss.
I don't know which is more right –
                              I like shortbreads as well as con carnes.

  But still not sure about the importance of scale. I don't know anyone who
has been to Bolivia, yet there are parts of my arm I don't notice everyday.

      Although recently: I was at lunch.
The dog from up the road looks to me before her invasion.

      She has come down from up the road to the *Silver Lounge* to scrounge
food from the old boys. I was eating Bombay mix and looking closely at the
capillaries on their faces.
I said I would use my mother's grandfather's filmcamera to make a film of
her.

Bela Tarr of Orpington! Ron Fricke of Kent!

But then I thought NO – something new shouldn't appear in old forms.
It all should be collected and held together fresh and new. A dogfilm
would have to be a dogfilm.
      Shona mbira of Zimbabwe
      Hammered dulcimers in Sweden
      Khoomei in the steppes.

Could there be postal services in the steppes? Mail vans couldn't be red if there was.

So many unsuccessful deliveries:
    – my father did not fix the octamus prime whilst I was having the operation 'down below' like he promised.

– I remember waking up in blood in the hospital corridor after the septicaemia operation, too afraid to call for help.

Incredible number of instances!
    Flag of Norway, Toyin's recipe for yam breakfast. Answer to boardgame question you didn't know: CAPTAIN SCARLET.

– in my pocket is the pebble from near St. Bees. I've no idea how long it has been a pebble.

    It's there because last night I took it from next to my candle;
That was the worst thing about last night – a busy moth flew into the
                                                                    flame and only
half died – it took me ages trying to get it out and put an end to it.

    My belly felt funny; like our argument. You said "you are always
                                                                    talking".
I had my red spotted pants on.
Backwards and forwards.
The Korean mass games. Fluorescent bacteria in the fish of the oceans.
                                                    My pencil
shavings and this girl saying that "world music is gay"

"You stop grumbling" says my mother. "And stop playing with yourself".
    I was in the car pressed fast against the window – my beano stickers
were left in the old house.
    There always is something missing.

So I sit and try to think of things I cannot think of that are red.

D. J. Mills

MADE

Autumn sunlight in the plane tree lifts
Stooping with the weight of it all
The wiry light still springing through

The shadows blow against the wall
Though you've planned the end
And so shine with us

Sore eyes twisted
Far from neglect

The stars fade the days in chill contract

Stewart Conn

VISITATION

In pride of place on my work-surface
are an ink-well of weighted glass

and a black quill-pen, presented to me
when I left long-term employ:

a discarded life I heed less
and less, as the years pass.

But every so often with a hoarse *kraaa*
there squats on the sill a hoodie crow,

a gap in one wing where a primary
feather is missing. Teetering raggedly

it fixes me with a bloodshot eye
then flops, disgruntled, away.

Whether bent on repossessing
what belongs to it, or chastising

me for treating its lost quill
as simply a glossy symbol,

I see in it the beast
of conscience come home to roost.

The cat meantime sits by the fireplace,
content that nothing is amiss.

Essays

The *Poetry Review* Essay

CHRIS MOSS

Myth

In 1925, 26-year-old Jorge Luis Borges wrote one of his most memorable poems, "The Mythical Foundation of Buenos Aires":

> The first barrel organ teetered over the horizon
> with its clumsy progress, its *habaneras*, its wop.
> The cart-shed wall was unanimous for YRIGOYEN.
> Some piano was banging out tangos by Saborido.
>
> A cigar store perfumed the desert like a rose.
> The afternoon had established its yesterdays,
> And men took on together an illusory past.
> Only one thing was missing – the street had no other side.
>
> Hard to believe Buenos Aires had any beginning.
> I feel it to be as eternal as air and water.
>
> (tr. Alistair Reid)

The city was founded in the sixteenth century, and Argentine independence won in 1816, but this is a vision of a city being born right before the poet's eyes. The 1920s were boom years in Argentina – the *"años locos"* or "crazy years" of tango, the rise of the middle-classes, massive meat exports – but the poem exudes the longing of an elegy. In Spanish, soft sounds drift up and away, intangible, unrooted: *"Una cigarrería sahumó comó una rosa... La juzgo tan eterna como el agua y el aire"*. Buenos Aires was, though, the most solid and substantial aspect of Borges' life at the time – and a rare source of hope and inspiration in the daily round of despair.

This landmark poem was included in Borges' third slim volume of poetry, *San Martín Copybook*, published in 1929. That same year, Borges publicly abandoned poetry, telling the magazine *Literatura Argentina* that he preferred prose to poetry, and, according to Edwin Williamson, "resigned himself to a career as an essayist and cultural commentator". In fact he would return to poetry at intervals between 1930 and 1985, but won international fame as a master of prose fiction. Though there is no question that his poetry changed and evolved, Borges would often return to a limited number of central obsessions. His last poem, called simply "1985", shows Borges was still concerned with the problem of the patria and Argentina's capacity to be born anew. Argentina is, still, "Something dreamed of yet never made".

Edwin Williamson's biography, *Borges: A Life* (Viking, £25, ISBN 0670885797), supercedes previous efforts to describe and decipher the life of the enigmatic Argentine writer. James Woodall's *The Man in the Mirror of the Book* (1996) was a highly readable but somewhat rushed attempt to cash in on the tenth anniversary of the author's death; while Emir Rodríguez Monegal's *Jorge Luis Borges: A Literary Biography* (1978) was written for a captive Argentine market familiar with Borges' local status as a somewhat distrait intellectual and national hero. There are closer, more searching analyses of Borges' work and status in Spanish – in Argentina, a leftist faction of literary scholars have continually challenged Borges' politics and the critical hyperbole that has attended his work – but Williamson offers a broad, balanced appraisal of the writer and the life.

According to Williamson, the poetry-prose dichotomy was but one of many fundamental tensions in Borges' long life. Reviewing the Argentine literary scene in the late nineteenth century, he illustrates how Borges' generation inherited an almost Arnoldian idea of civilisation as a war between the gaucho and caudillos of the pampas on the one hand, and the intellectual elite of Buenos Aires on the other. This classic city-country formulation was explored by Domingo F. Sarmiento in his 1845 fictionalised history, *Facundo; or Civilisation and Barbarism*, a seminal work that influenced Borges and all the Latin American writers of his generation.

As an upper-class *criollo* (Argentine of European descent), the question of national identity was close to Borges' heart. In early poems such as "Rosas", "General Quiroga Rides to His Death in a Carriage" and "Conjectural Poem", he analyses his cultural inheritance through his heroic ancestors. Related to Borges through his maternal grandfather, Doctor Francisco Laprida was murdered in 1829 by gaucho militiamen:

> Bullets whip the air this afternoon.
> A wind is up, blowing full of cinders
> As the day and this chaotic battle
> Straggle to a close. The gauchos have won:
> Victory is theirs, the barbarians'.
> I, Francisco Narciso Laprida,

> … longed to be someone else, to weigh
> judgments, to read books, to hand down the law,
> will lie in the open out in these swamps…
> > ("Conjectural Poem", tr. Norman Thomas di Giovanni)

A lonely death out in the wilderness also stole Borges' paternal grandfather:

> Colonel Borges sadly crosses the plain.
> What closed on him, the Remingtons' crackle,
> What his eye took in, endless grazing land…
> In his epic world, riding on his horse,
> I leave him almost untouched by my verse.
> > ("Allusion to the Death of Colonel Francisco Borges (1833-1874)",
> > tr. di Giovanni)

Williamson's central thesis is that the legacy of these heroic ancestors produced in the young author a schizophrenia between the "sword of honour" of his mother's noble ancestors, and the dagger of manly courage, embodied by his father, a womaniser, socialite and aspiring writer.

I'm not convinced. Plausible as it is, this theory becomes a tic in this biography, and detracts from the subtler passions at work in Borges' work. For Borges was subject to a complex battery of influences. He was educated to read in English by his grandmother Fanny Haslam (widow of Francisco Borges) during his infancy, and bullying at school led to his being tutored at home. Raised by his mother to think of himself as an upper-class *criollo*, young "Georgie" was an overprotected, fragile child. Yet, the Borgeses lived in a large house located in Palermo, then a seedy neighbourhood on the outskirts of Buenos Aires. Here he was drawn to the antics of the local wannabe gangsters, the *compadritos* who flashed knives and practiced tango moves on the street corners.

A now forgotten poet, Evaristo Carriego, a friend of Borges' father, fired the young boy's imagination with verses about the daily life of the barrio (neighbourhood) and the liminal zone of the *arrabal* – the place where pampas met the fringes of the city. Carriego's "El alma del suburbio" (The soul of the suburbs) portrays a city on the edge of the plains beneath vast skies, peopled by murderers, drunks, bohemians and slum-dwellers. He captures the melancholy of a city full of lonely men, where only the music of a barrel organ passing through provides solace. But even that must move on: "After a waltz you will leave like a / sadness crossing the deserted street, / and there will be someone left standing in a doorway / looking at the moon" ("Has vuelto").

> There is resignation in Borges' verse, and rarely a sense of liberation; honour not rebellion; measured emotion and never ecstasy; and, fundamentally, literature instead of sex.

This unorthodox poetry of the urban margins provided an irreverent alternative to the gauchesque literature of the time, and gave Borges a counter-reading of culture to challenge the *criollo* countryside mediations of José Hernández' *El gaucho Martín Fierro* (1872, 1879), which was embraced as Argentina's "national epic" in the early 1900s.

Between the age of 15 and 25, Borges would leave Argentina to live in Geneva on two separate occasions, move homes across Europe, meet the Futurists, Dadaists and Ultraists of the Spanish avant-garde in Madrid, Seville and Mallorca. Williamson details this period and illustrates how the travelling gave Borges an education in bohemia and a taste for radical manifestos and factional "schools" of poetry. But it also turned him into a half-exile. On his returns to Buenos Aires in 1921, and finally in 1924, he was spiritually removed from the city, even while the place and its language were ineffably his own. He forged a rich poetic voice from this entrepot of influences and impressions, finding in Buenos Aires a living metaphor for cultural encounter and collision, and in its margins he discovered a locus for his own sense of exile.

After reading Joyce's *Ulysses*, he laid out a plan to endow his unknown city with a mythology, whence such masterful early poems such as "The Mythical Foundation…", "The Recoleta", "Unknown Street", "Sunset Over Villa Ortúzar", many minor evocations of patios, blank facades of houses, the southside of Buenos Aires, and, ultimately, the forging of connections between Argentine heroes and the streets – and monuments – that bear their names. But Borges was more than a topographer. In "The Cyclical Night", published in his first retrospective collection in 1943, Borges attempts a metaphysic of city life:

> I do not know if we will recur in a second
> Cycle, like numbers in a periodic fraction;
> But I know that a vague Pythagorean rotation
> Night after night sets me down in the world
>
> On the outskirts of this city. A remote street
> Which might be either north or west or south,

But always with a blue-washed wall, the shade
Of a fig tree, and a sidewalk of broken concrete.

This, here, is Buenos Aires. Time, which brings
Either love or money to men, hands on to me
Only this withered rose, this empty tracery
Of streets with names recurring from the past

In my blood: Laprida, Cabrera, Solera, Suárez…

Squares weighed down by a night in no one's care
Are the vast patios of an empty palace,
And the single-minded streets creating space
Are corridors for sleep and nameless fear.

(tr. Reid)

All Buenos Aires' streets – laid out on the colonial grid system in city blocks of a single hectare – look the same to the returning exile unsure how to navigate them. Yet he is stirred, moved by them. Borges oscillates between a mathematicians' interpretation of destiny and that of a dreamer or mystic: repeatedly he ascribes emotion or character to streets, plazas, walls, as if they are his sole companions.

This mindscape of the *suburbio* is constraining but safe. There is resignation in Borges' verse, and rarely a sense of liberation; honour not rebellion; measured emotion and never ecstasy; and, fundamentally, literature instead of sex. His poems of the city ask a single question, repeatedly: can a relationship with a locality save a man – from hysteria, passions, the sense of time passing, and what Borges called "the nothingness of personality"?

Borges would transfer these concerns to his prose. The same poetic landscape dominates "The Streetcorner Man" (original title: "El hombre de la esquina rosada"), the first short story Borges published, in 1930. Other stories of the early period are rich in local colour, and what is particularly noteworthy about Borges' opus is that he would come back to this territory of the "suburbia" in the 1960s. The hoodlums and malingerers of the margins resurface in *Dr Brodie's Report* (1971). But the teleology of the short story makes more of the sequence of events, and has to take on board the allegorical demands of prose – in the poems, cycles and stasis preclude movement or progression.

More significantly, and not always grasped by earnest decoders of his puzzling stories and *faux* essays or *ficciones*, Borges was essentially a poet when writing prose too. His passion for the pithy phrase, the conundrum, for maximum compression and concision, and for the music of narrative and the potency of the symbol, evince the mind of a poet. He also wrote many brief prose poems and in the 1960s told his best-known translator, Norman Thomas de Giovanni, that he considered himself first and foremost a poet.

♫

The titles of Borges' poems suggest a vast, eclectic range of interests – "Matthew XXV: 30"; "Camden 1892"; "Spinoza"; "Texas"; "Embarking on the Study of Anglo-Saxon Grammar". But this encyclopaedic allusiveness is one element of a big intellectual joke. "Matthew XXV: 30", for instance, opens with the lines:

> The first bridge, Constitución Station. At my feet
> The shunting trains trace iron labyrinths.
> Steam hisses up and up into the night,
> Which becomes at a stroke the night of the Last Judgment.
>
> (tr. Reid)

The conceit is startling – in a single "stroke" we rise up from the criss-crossing tracks to the heights of theological reflection. The same poem contains a litany of many of the items the Borges universe is built around: "Stars, bread, libraries of East and West, / Playing cards, chessboards, galleries, skylights, cellars…". Borges explains that things interfere with words, almost apologises for letting his own metaphors rule over the Biblical legend. The local and immediate inspires – and then limits – the reflection.

Even the most arcane pursuits somehow turn around an "aleph" of local identity. Borges' interest in Anglo-Saxon derived from a life-long meditation on roots. If Buenos Aires could not supply ancient histories – the Spanish, and then the national government had annihilated all Argentina's indigenous tribes and erased their culture – then Britain possibly could. Yet even here, "To a Saxon Poet" is a lamentation for a lost "imprint of your feet", for "things buried in oblivion". In his poems and essays, Borges always moves from the physical world to abstraction, and from a historical to a philosophical vision.

At the other extreme, Borges was not above reworking the most stereo-typical of local myths: tango. These translate badly and only the Spanish originals capture Borges', pleasure in song and sound – in "Milonga de dos hermanos" he parodies the national verse epic Martin Fierro:

Traiga cuentos la guitarra
De cuando el fierro brillaba,
Cuentos de truco y de taba,
De cuadreras y de copas,
Cuentos de la Costa Brava
Y el Camino de las Tropas.

Though he despised the sentimental tangos of the 1920s and 1930s (he called them, famously "the cuckold's complaint"), Borges happily played with the tango slang known as *lunfardo* – but even his jaunty couplets written to be played with the guitar in *Para las seis cuerdas* (1965) suddenly switch from streetwise narrative to the thought that "Time is / Oblivion and memory". Tango was for dancers: happiness, for Borges, was an abstract noun.

Borges spent his long life constructing a complex mythology that operates at many levels – as pornography, as iconography, as landscape and as liturgy. Instead of whores, brothels and silk stockings – the more obvious objects of desire for his father, and for all the single men of the port – Borges transmuted his personal eros into tigers, mirrors, streets and sunsets, compasses, labyrinths, books, daggers and literary personae. In his essays on Dante, he would argue that the Italian poet used *The Divine Comedy* to memorialise Beatrice and contemplate a re-encounter with her in the afterlife. But these essays also betray Borges' own attempts to justify his convoluted flight from reality to fiction and solipsism. He engineered in his verse a proximity to history, as if the Buenos Aires boulevardier invents the city as he walks it.

In the last poems, death creeps in, not as a tombstone or memorial but as an emotional experience. In a poem written a few days after his mother's death, "El remordimiento" ("Remorse") he thanks his parents for giving him an education that prepared him for "the risky and beautiful game of life" but admits he has sacrificed his own youth and energy to "the symmetrical

> Instead of whores, brothels and silk stockings – the more obvious objects of desire for his father, and for all the single men of the port – Borges transmuted his personal eros into tigers, mirrors, streets and sunsets, compasses, labyrinths, books, daggers and literary personae.

challenges of art, which weaves mere nothingness".

Williamson argues convincingly that Borges was consumed by solipsism when he was rejected by women. Borges' work – both prose and poetry – is unusually solipsistic – as if self is subject to some kind of centripetal mechanism. Doubles, ghosts, dead people, solitary figures, hermits, kings, libraries and men "suffering from unreality" dominate plots characterised by slow movement and inertia and – at the mental level – reflection and misunderstanding. The *edges* of self seem largely absent from his work, which opens up into pantheism. At the emotional level, Borges-poet is revealed as a man who feels reduced to being an everyman, a non-person; the poems provide comfort and solace to the lonely and the godless.

❧

The Argentine capital is an enigma – its streets are a rectilinear labyrinth (the ultimate Borges trope) of national heroes and Independence battles; architecturally, its colonial past is juxtaposed with a teeming, disorderly modern metropolis; tango is like a collective, rhythmic memory; Buenos Aires is remote from geopolitical centres, and lives in permanent tribute to Paris, London, Rome, Miami; suddenly, after miles of cement and asphalt, its vertical fictions collapse into the hope-sapping horizontal plain of the pampas. All these beguiling qualities, and many more, are exposed and often resolved in Borges' opus. Like Joyce to Dublin, Kundera to Prague, Dickens or Eliot to London, Borges is the ultimate ghost-companion in Buenos Aires. It is his absolute faith in the essences of place and his conflictive fixation with local colour that give his poetry universal value – it is his mastery of form and his delicate handling of his own poetic sensibility that make the poems seem inevitable, necessary. If it is "hard to imagine" there was once a universe without Buenos Aires, it is partly because the verses of Borges have given the city a life and soul in words.

❧

Revoke the Sponsors

PAUL QUINN

Bruce Andrews, *Lip Service*, Coach House Books, $22.95, ISBN 1552450635

There is something almost wilfully scandalous about Bruce Andrews, the most rebarbative and least assimilable of the poets associated with the Language movement, producing a "recasting" of so sacred and canonical a text as the *Paradiso*. "Official Verse Culture" (to employ a notorious term coined by Charles Bernstein, Andrews's co-editor of the influential poetics journal, $L=A=N=G=U=A=G=E$) would probably prefer to imagine him consigned to the receiving end of an updated *Inferno*, rather than moving into profane alignment with the poem which, for T. S. Eliot, represents "the highest point that poetry has ever reached or can ever reach". Nevertheless, *Lip Service* is nearly four hundred pages of uncompromisingly disjunctive poetry, purporting to be a "near translation" of the *Paradiso*. On a cursory reading at least, it seems as far away from it as one could possibly imagine.

What, then, does Andrews derive from Dante? At the micro-level he sporadically makes use of cognate or false friend relations with the orginal Italian. In this restricted sense, as Bob Perelman has pointed out, Andrews is more indebted to Dante than even a full-blown Dante aficionado like Pound, who used the categories of heaven and hell conceptually, but resisted this kind of sustained assonantal homage (another sense of lip service), which is more akin to Louis Zukofsky's "translation" of Catullus. There is a natural attraction to Dante the linguisitic innovator, as opposed to Dante the celebrant of heavenly hierarchy; the Dante who, faced with the unprecedentedly difficult task of describing paradise, produces puns, torqued grammar and neologisms – including the very verb "imparadises" ('mparadisa) that Andrews imports into his own linguistic heaven. *Lip Service* is similarly scattered with nouns used as verbs, verbs as nouns, portmanteau words and coinages.

Andrews gives an account of the genesis of the project in the essay collection, *Paradise & Method*. Over several years he collected material (found phrases, re-spliced from reading, eavesdropping, multi-media bombardment), which he transcribed onto cards of between one and twenty words, concentrating particularly on themes like love, erotic intimacy, and the body. He then combined this with a triadic structure (which prefigured and probably predisposed the attraction to Dante) initially designed for an essay project, *Tips for Totalizers*. This template was in turn transposed to a poem based on themes from the *Paradiso*, and originally making use of epistolary

form. The re-channelled material was organised around an explicitly Dantean frame, moving through ten planetary bodies (paralleling Cantos): Earth, Moon, Mercury, Venus, Sun, Mars, Jupiter, Saturn, Fixed Stars, and Primum Mobile. The epistolary aspect was later jettisoned, but shreds of it remain amidst the more alienated mode of *Lip Service*: the odd, unrequited "Dear...", for example, snagged on a barbed wire of non-sequiturs.

This is possibly the most fascinating and weirdly appropriate aspect of this intertextual encounter. Dante is one of the supreme poets of vocation, invocation, apostrophe. The *Paradiso* contains some of the most remarkable examples of direct address to the reader in all literature (for example, the famous opening of Canto II, "O voi che siete in piccioletta barca . . ." / " O you that in your little bark . . . ") In Dante's trickle-down model of perfection, living light streams from the "Idea" that is the Word; Christ, the second person of the Trinity. Andrews's poetry often explores the rhetorical possibilities of the second person rather than the lyric "I". He is intensely interested in how readers (or consumers; there increasingly being little difference the wrong side of paradise) are called from on high, by the vested interests congealed in discourse. In Althusserian terms, we are "hailed" and, by acknowledging that it is we who are hailed *(Who? Me?)*, confirmed as subjects. Subsequently, we are subjected (a pun dear to Andrews) to Ideology. Althusser famously calls this process "interpellation". *Lip Service* sometimes reads like a cut-up version of paradise where Louis Althusser rather than Thomas Aquinas is the principal intellectual eminence. Bizarre as that might sound, the conjunction of these apparently incommensurable universes is surprisingly effective and thought provoking.

Andrews's last long work, *I Don't Have Any Paper So Shut Up (or, Social Romanticism)*, can be read as his *Inferno*. In that volume, the reader is not so much addressed as abused. It is overloaded with what Perelman calls "attack phrases". The idea of a target audience is literalised. The commodity culture ventriloquised by the poet barks and rails and threatens us (compare Dante's Plutus in the *Inferno*, screaming in tongues). Andrews takes the syntax of consumerism and reveals the underlying aggression it conventionally conceals; he uses a found, recombined language, articulated in a way which retains late capitalism's remorseless energy, but redeployed so as to shock instead of seduce. The relationship between author and reader, hailer and hailed, is caricatured into that between vendor and customer, rewritten as S & M. "Gestalt Me Out!", "Make Your Customers Nauseous", "Oh, Glaze Me Big!", "Scrape Me Off!" are some of the attention-grabbing titles or first lines of poems included. Because the inscribed command structure in that volume is so horrible (". . . hey, fuckhead, this is art . . ."), we pause before assuming the stable identity usually required of us. *I Don't . . .* is a strangely compelling (rarely have the connotations of that word been so fully tapped) and hilarious volume: "... emotion lost its franchise, but gloating and silence / already want to get paid...".

If *I Don't*... can be read as Andrews's commodified *Inferno*, *Lip Service* gravitates toward what should offer an earthly paradise: love, intimate relations, sexuality. The poem seems preoccupied with how power is institutionalised (a far from un-Dantean preoccupation), inculcated in what Althusser calls Ideological State Apparatuses, and focuses especially on how such apparatuses penetrate even the most intimate and "natural" spheres ("if you work within the system, the system works within you..."). Sexuality in our epoch has itself become commodified, has become, Andrews writes in a related essay on sexuality, "less a site of *production* than a site of *consumption* . . . figuring prominently in a near-totalizing machine of social discourse . . floodlighting these privacies – leaving us with no haven in an artificial heart-*filled* world . . . " Encapsulating this in *Lip Service* is the portmanteau term "pornoptic", conflating pornography and optics, with an additional extended suggestion of panopticon; an allusion to Bentham's architectural model of total surveillance. Any vision of paradise dependent on contempo-rary found material must be refracted through a culture of ubiquitous, market-driven, denatured, sexuality: "...orgasm is a mushroom of merchandise...".

In this figuration of interpellation we respond to a wolf whistle. How do we answer the call?

what a cock salute! –

it means *never arising*, no lexicon

exceeds slush speed unnaturally

conscripted by it:

self, grammatical *faction*.........

The "cock salute" of the first line above, in context, seems to mean Pavlovian sexual response; sexuality regimented into a salute, a reflex of power. This is the dystopian side of the pornoptic through which we glimpse a false paradise. It is ultimately quietist; paradoxically, this response means "never arising". Hailed (formed) in the midst of our most intimate moments, the subject is "conscripted," a "self" corralled as if by a grammar, by a fiction hiding in fact. This is only one of numerous possible readings of this typical passage. Unlike the crude transmissions of the communication industries upon which Andrews obsessively draws (whatever the discursive form they take: propaganda, popular fiction, advertising, pornography), it encourages us to consider a wide repertoire of possibilities (as much sound-based as sense-based). Indeed, in *Paradise & Method*, paradise is defined as "a total repetoire of possibilities".

The passage above echoes an earlier part of *Lip Service* which contains the phrase, "Pensible, smoked out by / form in the shape of a rooster ...". Here is another characteristic use of neologism : does "pensible" pack "sensible" and "pensive" together, combining the resistant and acquiescent *(be sensible!)* aspects of the person hailed? Or is it a truncated form of "indispensible," reflecting in this truncation that no one actually is? Once more, we are given a figuration of the retiring subject in his private space of dreams (that refuge where identity is dispersed), being "smoked out" – interpellated – by form or formal address – naturalised here in the institutional wake-up call of the rooster. I hear in that call a distant echo of Thoreau's "chanticleer"; distant, as a transcendentalist utopia must be from Andrews's "transdescending" dystopia, where desire has been co-opted and drilled. "I do not propose to write an ode to dejection", Thoreau writes in *Walden,* "but to brag as lustily as chanticleer in the morning, standing on his roost, if only to wake my neighbors up." 150 years of American history and literature later, in *Lip Service,* even the roosters have a message from our sponsors.

Nevertheless, Andrews still strives to wake his readers up, to "revoke the sponsors" and remind us "to accept no discourse except love's." One section, "Sun 8", includes another comic rendering of interpellation, analogous in its pithy offensiveness to several in *I Don't Have Any Paper* – "yo, bedwetters!" – and proceeds with an outright refusal to acknowledge the dominant ideology's address:

> I would like to state quite clearly
> that I have no intention
> of responding to this –
> impregnate every caption
> with the sound of your ego
> voiding, the answer is no...
> (nobody says 'NO' any more, dear; do try to catch up)...
> synthesized fear invites me.

Nobody says "no" because to refuse the call of ideology is to lose one's stable identity, to be an ego voiding; which, in the material paradise of his poem, is what Andrews invites us to do, to be. The poem regularly deploys the prefix "re-"; encouraging the reader at various times to "revoke", "readdress", "reinterpellate". We are enjoined to refuse the approaches of synthesised fear and instead, as in the *Paradiso,* seize opportunities for true imaginative collaboration; to seek out new constellations of meaning after closely observing how signs operate within concentric circles of social context. *Lip Service* ends – or should that be begins? – with the words, "let's start all over stars".

Reviews

Burning a pink cadillac

Jeremy Reed, *Duck and Sally Inside*, Enitharmon, £8.95, ISBN 01904634036;
Heartbreak Hotel, Orion, £12.99, ISBN 0752851594

The point about photographs is to trap the invisible, not the visible. The cover of Jeremy Reed's new collection, *Duck and Sally Inside*, shows a piece of kitsch martyrdom from a Munich photographer, called "Homage to B Soubirous", civil name of Saint Bernadette of Lourdes, played by Jennifer Jones in *The Song of Bernadette*, itself the subject of an adulatory book of collage poetry by John Wieners, who is a key figure for Reed. Duck and Sally are two characters from a Velvet Underground song named "Sister Ray", on which the guitarist deliberately played loud to obscure the lyrics, so I can't tell you their story. The Song of Bernadette is about Jennifer Jones being bullied by Vincent Price ("*I am the Imperial prosecutor. Do you know what that means?*"), but sticking to her story about seeing the Blessed Virgin – the gem which Reed takes away is the notion of piercing loyalty to a story.

Reed, like J. G. Ballard and Iain Sinclair, first took popular culture as his starting-point, in order to get away from the didactic staple of English poetry, the porridge of authenticity. Over time, he has replaced a sense of ruin with cherishing. Defying the bureaucracy which deals with selves, he sprinkles blessings on Outsiders loyal to weird scenes – Ray and Sylvia went to photograph sites where radioactive creep is taking over and discovered soldiers "cleaning up on minority ethics". Jack and Jacky offer bespoke funerals for the inauthentic – "One was to be buried in a pink fridge", one baked into chocolates. The stories are modern and perverse and inspire a certain apathy. Fantasy and appliances appear everywhere, continuing David Bowie's futuristic "Drive-in Saturday", where couples, bored by sex, copy courting behaviour from ancient films. A personal appearance by J. G. Ballard on p. 51 allows us to speculate on *The Crystal World* as the origin of Reed's myth of metabolic dislocation: a novel where whole countries freeze as crystal, exanimate.

Reed's idea of poetry has always been largely shaped by glam rock and by Bowie's "Rock and Roll Suicide", which is about a burnt-out rock star. Now he has written *Heartbreak Hotel*, 200 poems about Elvis Presley as a burnt-out rock martyr. When I bought *Elvis: the Sun Sessions* in 1976, I had a friend who had a valve amplifier for playing 1950s rock and roll. In those days, transistor amps were for *hippies*. Teds were paying £120 for copies of "One Hand Loose" on 78. As a rockabilly purist, then, I have to admire Reed's unlikely attempt to build a whole chapel of pin-up vitrines, or soda straws through which the

Power jumps to touch us. Reed really is more interested by the subject than by himself. He does come up with new research. His engagement and formal creativity are stunning throughout. But *Heartbreak Hotel* could be better at one fifth the length: Reed is unable to get close to Presley, his polar opposite. Reed is not a redneck's redneck; he's some way short of a shit kicker. This said, the poem about Presley's car having a moody "on the road between Hope and Texarkana" around 1956 is brilliant –

> black smoke
> volcanoing upfront, the car on fire,
> their quick hands jettisoning instruments,
> ejecting cases, as they run for clear
> and watch the limo crumple into flames,
> a blue and orange surfing roar
> sheeting the bodywork
> ("Burning a Pink Cadillac")

Reed could write a doctoral thesis on fan magazines, and he can name every fabric and shade when he writes a thirty line poem about neckties. Elvis' minority ethic was rockabilly. The fiddly, erudite, dinky instrumental touches on 60s records like "Wooden Heart" are acknowledged to be the worst thing about Presley, and Reed's fidgety, mannered brilliance sounds like them. But then Reed adapts his house theme of metabolic displacement to Elvis' gluttony, and we get extraordinary poems:

> The man's a cheeseburger mausoleum,
> an appetent contortionist
> snake-bloated on cholesterol junk,
>
> intestinal-roomy as a silo
> housing a grain harvest: he'll eat his way
> through bear-sized stacks of burgers and French fries,
>
> a deconstructing monument
> of sinuous eddies in fat
> ("Junk-food Junkie")

Even more terrifying is "Juicy Lucy cannibalises Elvis", a base somatisation of living for ever, darkened with religious references.

Due to disaffection among his songwriters, there was a gay subtext to Elvis – "Jailhouse Rock", widely thought to be about *comrade loves of the incarcerated* – but Elvis didn't know it was there. John Cale said "I thought Elvis died when he heard my version of *Heartbreak Hotel*": Reed's vision of fat as feminising Elvis, just as his taste in clothes and interest in jewellery did, is new and deeply satisfying. Like so many 1960s housewives, Presley was preoccupied with fat, food, barbiturates, and shopping. Reed fits the King into a myth (from the Gnostic *Gospel of St Thomas*, originally, via Moorcock's *The Final Programme*) whereby the future will belong to androgynes. Life will go on through asexual means – viruses, clones, digital transcription, cryogenic suspension. Maybe a subculture which reproduces itself through photographs is like a crystal which grows in a solution. Maybe the crystals in Ballard's subjective landscapes are like the barbiturate downers which dominate the book – and Presley's life. Not a high, but a kind of apathy in which dreams were possible. A TV of the soul.

Reed himself became a poetic myth, a star crystal, and so went outside cellular time: after writing 2000 poems, where can you go? Perhaps these are Reed's Vegas years; benign, indulgent, glamorous, sophisticated, idling, while we recall his great days (circa *Bleecker Street, The Isthmus of Samuel Greenberg, Saints and Psychotics* and *Walk on Through*) when he was fired by more violent anxieties, going through more carnal transformations.

ANDREW DUNCAN

Modem poetry

Richard Price, *Lucky Day,*
Carcanet, £8.95, ISBN 1857547616

Lyric poetry is the art of self-perceiving speech. Whatever phenomena a lyric poem perceives in the external world – the small rain, a summer's day, a red wheelbarrow – its primary perception is of itself, as a voice feeling its way through the fact of versification.

There is a modern misconception, however, that lyricism is primarily perception of externals, subsequently versified. The Imagism of Ezra Pound is still misunderstood in this respect. Pound's 1913 poem "In a Station at the Metro" ("The apparition of these faces in the crowd; / Petals on a wet, black bough.") is often quoted as an example of how important the surprising comparison is to the modern poet. But the bleary conceit that in some way faces in a crowd resemble petals on a bough – the visual image – is really the least important element of that lyric; it is only the occasion to present the emotional image of a speaker discovering, in speech, the total momentary insight – "*these* faces" – as significant. The poem does not present a verifiable simile, but a voiced, unparaphrasable apprehension. It does not mistake the original connection alone for the modern emotion.

Informationism, the Scottish poetry movement of which Richard Price was part in the early 1990s, did at times make this mistake in its desire to discover a notionally modern poetics. Take, for example, the similes of Robert Crawford's "Scotland" – "Optoelectronics of hay" – or Price's own "An informationist's kitchen" (1994): "Stacked like DATs / there are flapjacks with millennial dates". In these poems the technologised world is noticed from an ironic pastoral or domestic distance. In Price's kitchen, awareness of the abstract science of data storage has an ironically concretising effect: the dimensions of a flapjack do resemble a Digital Audio Tape cassette, while the sound-pattern of "stacked", "DATs", and "-jacks" adds an audible crunch to the image. The sound effects, though, are just that – enhancements of a prose witticism, uncoordinated by feeling. The lines play with the sights and sounds of the information era, but with little sense of themselves as feeling speech formed by its conditions.

That was eleven years ago. Reflecting on the poem recently, Price has written that the style of "An informationist's kitchen" might be read as a "parody" of a magazine article describing modern domestic space. In the best poems of *Lucky Day* – a gathering of several small collections and sequences written since – he achieves a more sophisticated lyricism of the information age. Like the later poetry of Craig Raine – whose early "Martianism" clearly informs the perceptive estrangements of the Informationist poems quoted above – *Lucky Day* develops a sparer, finer sense of hesitation and repetition as effective lyric devices in themselves. This upgraded, broken-down Informationism apprehends that there is no valid parodic distance between lyrical speech and functional English; it discovers in the language and condition of information the language and condition of emotion.

Price's nimble similes are still in evidence – "On the stereo / a single's black coffee / twirls its central cream" – but they are not a stylistic staple. Instead, the facts of modern life are selectively arranged to reveal their own strangeness – as in this image from *Hand Held*, a sequence about a daughter with severe learning difficulties: "in the Inn at the Zoo /… / …the gargling / electronic cockatoo / in the rafters / above the ketchup". The structural concomitant of the witty simile, a kind of rational riddling about the occasion of a poem, can still upset the lyric balance though, punch-lining otherwise open-ended arrangements of images with meaningful nudges: "like a love-letter // we fold the bed-cover".

All good lyric poetry, from A.E. Housman to J. H. Prynne, is obscure (intellectual content is another question), because the self-perceiving speech of lyric is only interested in the elaboration of an emotion, not its occasion. The opening section of *Lucky Day* – "Scape" – goes successfully further in trusting to the lyric sufficiency of such obscurity. Several poems recall the spare found-speech-and-object arrangements of the American Language poet Rae Armantrout, in which the lyric emotion is patterned across the scattered parts of the whole. The reader is given emotional information, not analysis. The most exemplary new Informationist lyric collected here, though, comes in the later section, *A News*. "Softened, bright" first appeared in *Poetry Review* in Spring 2003; since then, Price has subtly revised it for even greater concision:

> Computer light improves any painting,
> back-lit for a radiant show.
> Vermeer's balance, even,
> glistenises, remains in its glisten.
>
> The casual folds – those drapes –
> stay, too, but know fabric now
> as memories can think they know
> what was best, what was
> likely true.
>
> Back-lit for a virtual exhibition:
> I haven't a single picture of you
> (days that did know what a day was),
> can't now.
>
> Softened, bright.
> It's so good to have the,
> to have the technology.

Every line of "Softened, bright" is self-perceiving, lyrical speech; an occasion may easily be inferred around the poem (speaker views Vermeer's "Woman Holding a Balance" on the Internet, recalls old flame) but the poem itself only speaks of immediate perceptions: the visual clarity of digitised technology, the nature of memories. The colloquial musical awkwardness of the vocabulary ("glistenise"), grammar ("what was / likely true"), rhyme and repetition is a far lyric cry from flapjacks-stacked-like-DATs, but a much truer and more touching account of connection and disconnection in the age of modems.

JEREMY NOEL-TOD

Undercover prying

Adrienne Rich, *The School Among the Ruins: Poems 2000–2004*
Norton, $22.95, ISBN 0393059839

In her latest collection Adrienne Rich continues to mix the personal with the political, touching on subjects ranging from 9/11 to the Iraq war to the ongoing Israeli/Palestinian conflict. Rich is well known in the States for her engagé stance on progressive issues; her writings, both poetry and prose, frequently address sexism, homophobia, racism and social inequality in America. As a voice against oppression, whether at home or abroad (including that visited by her homeland abroad), she has spent much of her life in protest. Yet to categorise Rich as simply a political poet is to underestimate her considerable artistry – the music and mystery of her words – as well as the scope and variety of her project.

To Rich, now in her seventies, poetry may still be that "old subversive shape", a site for investigating "*the history / of torture*" under Pinochet or the uprisings of "May '68", but it's also a space for memorialising lost friends and expressing love for her partner. Even more striking, Rich engages in a surprising amount of metaphysical speculation throughout this volume, worrying the "skeins of consciousness" to fascinating ends. Pieces like "Equinox" and "Trace Elements", with their use of empty spaces separating phrases, erratic line indentations, and fragmented repetitions, look, and sound, like mid-period Jorie Graham. The sense of urgent interrogation ("Can say I was mistaken?"), of thought enacted on the page in heightened utterance ("her only   now   seeing it   [only now]"), that marked *The End of Beauty* is also to be found here, along with the exquisitely physical, felt images: "the spine's vertical necklace swaying", "the collarbone's reverberant line".

Rich subtly ponders the nature of perception in these lyrics, while also exploring the idea of memory, which "pursues its errands" more insistently the older we get. Memories are "small clear refractions / from an unclear season", which act by salvaging bits of the author's consciousness from the murky depths of her past. This is another form of diving into the wreck, only this time Rich seeks to retrieve not feminist history but her own former selves. The passing of years haunts poems such as "Alternating Current", a sequence of elliptical scenes from the past ("Take one, take two / – camera out of focus"), which are, crucially, re-viewed from the present ("take three"). Rich's awareness of ageing, of an ever changing self, is both poignant and poised: "We remain or not but not remain / as now we think we are". But when death – "the faint clockface" – keeps looming nearer, how is the poet to "slow the hemorrhaging" of existence? Though Rich cites the usual credo of the writer (I will live on through my words), she seems rather to accept mortality than defy it. "When our late grains glitter / salt swept into shadow / . . . will it matter?" Not, she suggests, as long as "there's tenderness and solidarity" left in the world.

If tenderness and solidarity sound too hippie-ish, Rich's more overtly political poems add depth to her world view. In the book's third section, "Territory Shared", she combines references to Israel's occupation of the West Bank and Gaza Strip with an extended meditation on language. (The section's title comes from an epigraph by the Bakhtinian semiotician V. N. Volosinov, which runs in part: "Each and every word expresses the 'one' in relation to the 'other' . . . A word is territory shared by both . . . the speaker and his interlocutor".) In "Transparencies", Rich moves from the guilt publicly expressed by some Israeli soldiers – "word that [they hope] would cancel deed" – to a series of metaphors likening language to glass.

Words are "windowpanes in a ransacked hut, smeared", but also "clear as glass till the sun strikes it blinding". A word "can be crushed like a goblet underfoot", or "can translate into broken bones". (The goblet line alludes to the ceremonial breaking of a wine glass by the bride and groom at traditional Jewish weddings.) Through such images Rich shows words to be obfuscatory, dangerous, deceptively double-edged – far from shared territory. Yet despite the failure of language to cancel deeds already done, there's a possibility of redemption: "in a dark windowpane you have seen your face / . . . when you wipe your glasses the text grows clearer". What counts, it seems, isn't only what one says, but how one understands the words said by others. Even then, in Rich's implacable logic, a shared understanding, a shared territory, isn't enough to save us. It comes down to what we do, or don't do – "how you live it". If "word and body / are all we have to lay on the line", then words can't be separated from actions; both are needed to achieve justice.

Other pieces, though effective, offer more-predictable responses to recent events. "Don't Take Me" is a satire on the right-wing climate of suspicion and violation of civil liberties in the States following 9/11; "The Eye" is an elegiac farewell to normal life during times of conflict, whether in America, Afghanistan, the Middle East or the former Yugoslavia. At times Rich lets her good intentions run away with a poem, as in the collection's title sequence, another war-is-bad lament. But at her finest, what she calls her "undercover prying" still feels fresh – no small feat given the tendency of many established writers to grow stale. In this volume, by extending her enquiries into new terrain (philosophical, psychological), Rich has revitalised her work. That "music from a basement session overheard" sounds sweeter than ever.

JANE YEH

Criminal records

Sinéad Morrissey, *The State of the Prisons*,
Carcanet, £6.95, ISBN 1857547756

Sinéad Morrissey's third collection opens and closes with a dramatic monologue. The first, "Flight" (see p. 35 of this issue), is in the urgent voice of a woman who has been publicly gagged; the second is that of John Howard, prison reformer, whose 1777 treatise provides the title both for this collection and for the long poem which forms the second part of the book. Elsewhere we are treated to vignettes of W. H. Auden and Alexander the Great, together with a mischievous piece of rhyming "Advice" to fellow poets ("Don't be proud / Viciousness in poetry isn't frowned on, it's allowed"). The book also features commentaries on recent political events, and accounts of journeys abroad (to China, New Zealand, and Germany, continuing a "travelogue" theme that has run through both of Morrissey's previous collections), together with lyrics on the more personal history of childhood and early adulthood. It's a very broad range of subject matter, marshalled, for the most part, into exquisitely crafted poems.

"The State of the Prisons" is written in six-line stanzas with a strict rhyme scheme which Morrissey sustains over six pages. The form propels the narrative and her fluent recreation of the eighteenth-century voice of John Howard:

> The prisoners entered, pulling on long chains.
> A muscle jerked in my thumb. The judge was eminent,
> Bored, ecclesiastical, inured to the stench of sweat and excrement
> That flowered where they stood. I was reeling back to a stone hole
> And darkness interminable, as the felons' crimes
> Were pronounced against them in a nasaloid drone.

Howard was a devout man, a teetotaller and non-conformist. But running parallel to the account of his social reform work is the tragedy of his personal history: the death of his wife and the slow corruption of his son (sent away to school by Howard at the age of four and neglected thereafter). The two stories throw up arresting questions about faith, and the sacrifice required for public life, even the nebulous reasons by which someone might embark on this path.

"The State of the Prisons" works as a self-contained narrative – there is no overt attempt to link it with contemporary events, although the description of "shackles" and the conditions in which prisoners were held inevitably brings them to mind. Morrissey does, however, tackle more recent history in "The Wound Man" and "Migraine". In the former she alludes to Lorca's *Poet in New York*, looking back at the poet in the city at the time of the Wall Street crash and then fast-forwarding to the collapse of the twin towers: "Had you survived . . . / Between that fall of faith and this, what would you think? / Would you know what has happened here, / the way we do not know what has happened?" She finishes by envisioning the Wound Man (an early medical diagram of a man studded with a variety of weapons and the wounds they inflict) stalking the streets of America. It's a characteristically nightmarish image that powerfully evokes the sense of something huge and bleak having been unleashed. In "Migraine" she places the narrator inside the Moscow theatre siege and gives her a debilitating migraine through which to describe it. The fractured reality that results strongly conveys the shock of experiencing events which were previously inconceivable:

> . . . My awful light. Light in the wrong place.
> Like the sun at midnight or blood on the moon's face.

This poem, and others – such as "Zero" ("it lived . . . / in the kiss of a thumb and forefinger / in the sigh at the bottom of a poured-out water jar"), and "The Gobi From Air" ("Auden's face in age / looked like this place") – are full of imaginative detail. In contrast to these, however, the portraits of elderly friends or relatives ("Aunt Sarah's Cupboards") and an account of time spent abroad ("Juist") seem over-explained. In "Juist", the authorial "I" is too prominent and the long lines seem to want to revert into a prose memoir. It's interesting to note that in this poem Morrissey returns to a scene which is also described in her first collection, *There Was Fire in Vancouver*. In that book, the phosphorescent sea symbolises a moment of transcendence ("it is as though God said / Let there be light"); here however, it is a mere backdrop to the narrator's state of mind:

> . . . waves, peeling
> apart from themselves, hurled phosphorescent plankton into visual ecstasy . . .

> *And all this for me.*

Another motif continued from *There Was Fire in Vancouver* is evident in the poems which engage with iconic poets from the twentieth century. As well as the tongue-in-cheek "Advice", there's a poem which revels in the "avoidable mistakes" of "Larkin on Empire, say, or Plath on Aunts". These are fun, but I can't see how the modern variation of Frost's "Stopping by Woods on a Snowy

Evening" adds anything new to a reading of the original, no matter how faithful it is to Frost's rhymes and metre. Perhaps this is because it seems too much like an exercise around a well-worn theme, whereas the monologues that engage with history and place transport the reader to exhilarating new territory. The more challenging the subject matter, the more precise Morrissey's language becomes

JANET PHILLIPS

✑

Disfiguring splendours

Geoffrey Hill, Scenes from Comus,
Penguin, £9.99, ISBN 0141020237

Geoffrey Hill is a quick poet. He is quick in the sense that, as everyone seems now to recognise, no writer approaches Hill in being so alive to, and alive in, the language. The reason for this is not the perverse and self-aggrandising will to obscurity of which Hill has on occasion been accused, but because the difficulty of living demands an answering difficulty in the words of great writers, a seemingly intolerable burden placed on the staggeringly gifted: as Hill puts it, in a single line of characteristic concentrated reflection in *Scenes from Comus*, "That weight of the world, weight of the word, is". Hill is quick, too, in that, in recent years, one astonishing collection has rapidly followed another: so *Scenes from Comus* has already ceded its place as the latest of Hill's works to *A Treatise of Civil power* just published by the Clutag Press. Hill, then, is too quick for his reviewers, the present writer included, but this is merely a fact which assures painstaking readers – "the learned readers of J. Milton" and, one adds, of G. Hill – of more enduring rewards. T. S. Eliot's notion that "genuine poetry can communicate before it is understood" is, taken out of context, a dangerous formulation, vulnerable to misappropriation in justifying the unintelligible and the unintelligent. Nonetheless, long before Hill's poems are fully understood, it is already clear that *Scenes from Comus* is exceptionally and truly important, a work of breathtaking concentration.

    Scenes from Comus is dedicated to Hugh Wood on his seventieth birthday. The musician, Hill's friend and exact contemporary, composed his own *Scenes from Comus*, a symphonic cantata, in the early 1960s. So Hill, Wood and Milton keep company here, as Hill acknowledges in a moment of generous and affectionate wit:

> He [Milton] was a cheerful soul and loved your music,
> Hugh, as he must have told you many times.

Scenes from Comus is about the English Civil War and Hill's England, the England of the Severn, the border with Wales, Ludlow. It stops over, as Hill himself is wont to do, in Reykjavik in mid-Atlantic, the wintry Atlantic of the Second World War. It is about music and painting, masquing and masking, guising and clowning. Like Milton's *Comus* it is about sexual passion. It is about ageing. In this collection, all such matters reflect on one another in varying, astonishing ways.

However, the initial question to ask of *Scenes from Comus* concerns its style, its distinctive way of thinking and feeling. There is certainly continuity here with the continuous yet continually self-interrupting style of earlier volumes: "What / a weirdo, you think. Well, yes, I was wired weird." Clearly, then, weightiness does not exclude humour, and Hill's unsettled and unsettling style is intent neither to "wax portentous" nor to "quip it away". With *Scenes from Comus*, however, that style has become more abrupt, a poetry of stops and starts, turns and returns: the poetic voice here has something of the clipped, curt, thinking-on-its-feet immediacy of Senecan prose style.

In this collection Hill twice quotes Milton's *"In Wintry solstice like the shorten'd light"*. The source is not in this case *Comus* but "The Passion", a poem which Milton left unfinished because – ironically in this new Hillian context – Milton judged the subject to be beyond his years. Shortening is much in evidence in *Scenes from Comus*. The collection divides into three sections: "The Argument of the Masque", twenty poems of ten lines each; a central section of eighty poems, "Courtly Masquing Dances", where the poems are especially short, either nine or seven lines in length; and "A Description of the Antimasque", a further twenty poems, each twelve lines long. Units of syntax, and thus of sense here, are also characteristically short, sometimes not even filling the whole single line. *Scenes from Comus* again evinces that extraordinary physicality of language which we associate with Hill, and here in these short days – "our short days", "these latter days", "the short day", "a hand's span / from the end of time", "short arctic days", "the last days" – Hill is much concerned with breath since, as he succinctly tells us, "Inspiration breathes hard". Breathing hard, then, Hill figures himself as being sea-sick in rough seas (the sea being a literal and figurative concern throughout this collection) describing how "the deep waters toss me about – I shout / from the crests and the troughs". Readers must anticipate being similarly pitched around.

So far this description might suggest that *Scenes from Comus* is fragmented, or tending to break up. On the contrary, it is highly concentrated:

no sooner is something said but Hill's verse turns back upon itself and intensifies itself. The stylistic means by which such concentration is effected is rhyme, for in *Scenes from Comus* rhyme too might be described as having shortened, moving in from the line-ending to work internally, often completing its effect within the single line. In its "purest" form such rhyming involves twinning, the immediate repetition of a word or phrase in a mirroring reflection. (Mirrors too are a recurrent concern in these poems, appositely so in a work Hill himself describes as a "mono-duet"; a work densely concerned with reflection in the many senses of that word; a work looking back on former selves; and a work dedicated to a close friend and fellow artist.) Examples of such rhyming are everywhere in the collection: "of character as self-founded, self-founding", "at once rational, irrational", "which may be now, might very well be now", "Rain-front on rain-front", "I see the pristine hammer hammer alarm".

Hill himself, again too quick for his critics, describes and simultaneously enacts all that I have been trying to elucidate here, in altogether more succinct and clear fashion when he writes

Give me a break
in concentration, só I can concentrate, …

In *Scenes from Comus* this stylistic concentration mirrors a concentration (a concise intensity) of thinking and feeling. For example, ageing is one of Hill's concerns here, a large area of human experience which Hill has already tackled in ways which rival Samuel Beckett at his finest and most testing. In *Scenes from Comus*, Hill again does not shrink from depicting the awfulnesses of ageing and illness. He does surprise us, however, in reflecting how the debilitations of age are experienced, not as diminutions, but as intensifications and he writes of his intention to "praise autumn's / dense clearances, its disfiguring splendours", phrases which are themselves dense and ambiguous oxymorons, part of Hill's "grand and crabby music". So, for example, what we unthinkingly – and unfeelingly – might describe as ear trouble is given deafening realisation:

my other pulse, beating to Plato's rhythm
heard through circadian circuits of distress.
Loud hissing in the ears may or may nót
mean blood pressure soaring, or sex on heat,
or siren voices, or yr lisping snakes.

Eye trouble is evoked in another poem (Hill having told us

self-deprecatingly, glancing at the Christmas cliché, that "These short ones are the sock-fillers"):

> A fish-shaped embryo aureoled in flame
> glows from the time-scarred retina's
> scratch kaleidoscope. A thing even of beauty
> I fancy – ánd less strange than goldfish
> on black and white TV. Now Piscis breaks
> out into floated plaques and warps of colour.
> I'll join you – wobbly swimmers of the eye!

Hill remarks how "Even short arctic days have a long twilight // as I have time to observe" and presents such experiences unsentimentally, as likely to be nightmarish as they are to be a cause for celebration. Less always threatens to be more, and, faced with the seeming paucity of the Icelandic vista, Hill can seem exasperated by the power of the imagination:

> Four days on floor six of the Radisson
> Saga | and thís had to happen: high density,
> high intensity spaces
> of imagination…

Reviewers wrenching gobbets from the body of a collection cannot but misrepresent such work, but it is the duty of reviewers to encourage readers to read good, indeed, great, writing. In this context, perhaps the fourteenth poem of the first section of *Scenes from Comus* may stand in isolation and yet convey the distinctive qualities of Hill's work. Moreover, here Hill helps us, as he often does, telling us who he is quoting and what they are writing about:

> *Not in these noises* – Milton. *A troubled sea*
> *of noises and hoarse disputes*, is also him.
> Even short arctic days have a long twilight
>
> as I have time to observe. Gloam lies pulsing
> at the sea-skyline, where the *Hood* blew up
> surging at full speed, a kind of wake
>
> over the sudden mass grave foul with cordite,
> gradually settling. Milton meant civil war
> and civil detractions, and the sway of power,
>
> the pull of power, its *pondus*, its gravity.

Milton's figurative sea encloses the literal sea of the Second World War, each conflict reflected on the other. The concentrated image at the poem's centre is of the exploding HMS *Hood*, speedily forming its own wake, in a self-inwoven image suggestive of similar conceits in the poetry of the English Civil War – Marvell's drop of dew, for example, "Like its own tear". "Grave" and "gravity" come alive hideous Irony – in the fullness of their various meanings, and the true weight of that seemingly casual, seemingly reassuring, phrase, "gradually settling", unsettles us. Geoffrey Hill is a quick poet.

JOHN LYON

Terrible counterparts

Barry MacSweeney, *Horses in Boiling Blood: MacSweeney, Apollinaire: a collaboration, a celebration*, Equipage, ISBN 1900968762

Horses in Boiling Blood is announced as the last book completed by Barry MacSweeney before his death in 2000. Its publication follows the recent appearance of *Wolf Tongue: Selected Poems 1965-2000* from Bloodaxe, which includes *The Book of Demons, Postcards from Hitler*, and *Pearl in the Silver Morning*, all completed during the period of this book's composition between May 1997, when MacSweeney visited Paris, and his death. It collects MacSweeney's "collaboration" with, and celebration of, Apollinaire, and frequently the later, wartime Apollinaire at that: some are "after Apollinaire", others "inspired by Apollinaire [or Guillaume]", and one, "Letter from Guillaume Apollinaire to Barry MacSweeney", arrives directly from "In the trenches". War's shadows are cast long all around, so that while some of Apollinaire's pre-1914 work ("Zone", "La Chanson du Mal Aimé", "Annie") acquires references to the trenches, other poems are darkened by images of the Second World War and the conflict in Iraq. Perhaps this is partly an attempt to deal with Apollinaire's great enthusiasm for war, by acknowledging through a widened lense the disparity between the bright technological future for which the soldier-poet had hoped to clear a path and the terrible century of murderous technocrats that actually followed. Yet MacSweeney intensifies some of the most uncomfortable parts of the performance (and both poets are great limelight-grabbing performers): horses originally in a frieze (trees in No Man's Land "ragged to ribbons" by artillery) are here boiled in blood, while the "ardeurs de géhenne" ("ardours of Gehenna") in "In Charge Of The

Lads" ("Chef de Section") are now "the arduous wonders of genocide".

As this might suggest, the poems are more often free renderings than straight translations. Many of them in fact depart very far from their beginnings in Apollinaire, who like Laforgue before him has been better served by being lifted into new poems than by translation. The most successful adaptation of Apollinaire's tone, movement and cadence to English has been in the poetry of Frank O'Hara rather than the several editions of *Alcools* and *Calligrammes* now available, and *Horses in Boiling Blood* frequently echoes the American poet too. The title of MacSweeney's version of "La Porte", "Entrance to Heaven", surely refers to O'Hara's "Rhapsody", with its "door to heaven? portal / stopped realities", and that poem, closing as it does with an abrupt, apocalyptic evocation of "the enormous bliss of American death", is a suitable intermediary for two poems that link enigmatic doorways and apprehensions of mortality. On the other hand, O'Hara is probably also responsible for this:

> I questioned – on the first time we made love – whether you
> trimmed your quim hair and you said no –
> And I have always thought you a complete idol ever since

However, what MacSweeney, Apollinaire and O'Hara share above all is a conception of lyric that combines an improvisatory dedication to the moment and the attempt to will the self to presence (and permanence) through a foregrounded and highly personal address to a network of lovers, friends, fellow poets and predecessors, always interrupted by thoughts of death. In *Horses in Boiling Blood*, Apollinaire's songs of his wartime self become subject to MacSweeney's own personalising will: the moment of encounter with the original poems sparks a series of associations and memories of other encounters. The poet wanders the 20th arrondissement or drives a 2CV illegally down the byroads, goes shopping or for coffee, writes to Jackie, or remembers a journey to Scotland with J. H. Prynne, and the war or the death of friends intervenes. This is the source of both the greatest successes and the most regrettable failures in this book. It produces the most poignant moments, such as the Villonesque epitaph "The Dollbird/Redblonde", where the shrapnel wound and trepanning of Apollinaire's skull that came to haunt the last poems of *Calligrammes*, and which weakened the poet and contributed to his death from flu, find their terrible counterpart in MacSweeney's memory of "the Heminevrin drip". The "Letter From Guillaume Apollinaire to Barry MacSweeney" ends as it opens on to our time:

> My fellow poet
> don't despair at the non-appearance of your book

you know that it will appear one day
We may both be dead
but the lights in the sky
and the brilliant shadows under the wheels
of these tremendous modern cars

However, there is sometimes the suspicion that war too easily forms for MacSweeney a suitably apocalyptic backdrop to love poems, the fractured sentimentality of which might otherwise pall. Too many of these poems lose the force and shape of Apollinaire's originals, becoming simple pegs on which to hang the poet's obsessions and his chauvinism. For confirmed fans of MacSweeney, this book remains valuable as a glimpse of the poet confronting a major influence, but readers new to his work should still head straight for *Wolf Tongue*, and in particular *Pearl* and *The Book of Demons*. There they will find the "mercy ache tenderness / Unbelievable sanity" to which his best poems are promised.

MALCOLM PHILLIPS

All styles recommended

Richard Wilbur, *Collected Poems 1943–2004*,
Harcourt, $35, ISBN 0151011052

Besides the Richard Wilbur that all serious American, and many British, readers know, there are at least four others no one talks about. The familiar Wilbur presents a technically flawless paradigm of dignified, mostly stanzaic, mostly rhyming verse, much of it devoted to beautiful forests, statuary, easel paintings, married love and parenthood, a paradigm to which young poets disenchanted with recent styles resort: this Wilbur detects "a poignancy in all things clear", likens poets to architects and jugglers, and advises that "a heaven is easier made of nothing at all / Than the earth regained". This Wilbur is real, valuable, and at least as talented as his acolytes suggest. But there are others, all valuable in themselves. This hefty *Collected Poems* (his third overall, his first since 1987, and the first to include his verse for children) offers the juggler-architect along with: a shocked (even shell-shocked) American soldier; a fiercely partisan political liberal; a versatile translator; and a thoughtful, almost Hardyesque singer of subdued grief.

Take the beautiful craftsman first. This is the once-influential, easily-caricatured Wilbur who dominates *Ceremony* (1950) and *Things of This*

World (1956); when Randall Jarrell wrote that too many 1950s poets "came out of Richard Wilbur's overcoat," or distinguished him from imitators by writing that Wilbur himself "obsessively sees, and shows, the bright underside of every dark thing", it's this Wilbur whom Jarrell had in mind. Rarely have vowels and consonants seemed so purely melodic, nor so expertly managed, as in "A Storm in April", perhaps the best of Wilbur's many seasonal set-pieces:

> This storm, if I am right,
> Will not be wholly over
> Till green fields, here and there,
> Turn white with clover,
>
> And through chill air the puffs of milkweed hover.

If he would avoid monotony, a poet devoted to perfection of form must also devote himself to variety, and so Wilbur's collections double as sparkling cyclopedias of forms and subgenres – not just sonnets and villanelles but taut quatrains, couplets of all sorts, Provençal ballades, flawless terza rima, comically polysyllabic exact rhyme, lyric dialogue, aubade, Anglo-Saxon accentual metres ("Lilacs", "Junk"). His pastoral love poems even boast actual pastures:

> You, in a green dress, calling, and with brown hair,
> Who come by the field-path now, whose name I say
> Softly, forgive me love if also I call you
> Wind's word, apple-heart, haven of grasses.

For all his appreciation of conventionally admirable things ("A Baroque Wall-Fountain in the Villa Sciarra," various temperate-climate trees, his wife) some of his triumphs in praise-poetry concern things and events few others would notice:

> So that when somebody spoke and asked the question
> Comment s'apelle cet arbre-là?
> A girl had gold on her tongue, and gave this answer:
>> Ça, c'est l'acacia.

Wilbur's introduction to Europe came at a decidedly less golden moment: he served with the US Army in World War Two, and drew fire near Monte Cassino, "living in a hole on a hillside subject to harassing artillery fire," as he recalled in 1995. Like other Cold War poets (but slightly earlier, and to better effect), Wilbur saw the beauties of postwar France and Italy – from the cedilla to the Villa Sciarra – through a wartime lens. No one should read Wilbur's first book, *The Beautiful Changes* (1947), without seeing how often it evokes 1943 and '44. In "Mined Country", "boys come swinging slow over the grass", gracefully manipulating not baseball nor cricket bats but metal detectors. The "night guard" in "First Snow in Alsace" loves how the new flakes muffle the recent deaths:

> Absolute snow lies rumpled on
> What shellbursts scattered and deranged,
> Entangled railings, crevassed lawn.
>
> As if it did not know they'd changed,
> Snow smoothly clasps the roofs of homes
> Fear-gutted, trustless and estranged.

War service informs Wilbur's sense (which Jarrell scanted) that we need all the effort of intellect, aesthetic detachment and studied technique to stem the panic in our wounded hearts. "Man Running" imagines the day when proto-people first "descended from the trees / Into the shadow of our enemies, / Not lords of nature yet, but naked prey". "A Barred Owl" depicts a negative apotheosis of supposed innocence, "A small child . . . dreaming of some small thing in a claw/ Borne up to some dark branch and eaten raw".

Wilbur lauds self-restraint, sociability, charity, and views with suspicion all violence, all aggression, and all crowds (his "nature" is almost the inverse of D. H. Lawrence's); Western civilization seems to Wilbur an impressive, though bloody and clearly imperfect, inheritance. In other words, he's a stalwart American liberal, concerned about the tyranny of the majority, protective of civil liberties, and generally opposed to invading small countries, Vietnam very much included. As the American critic James Longenbach has, almost alone, pointed out, Wilbur's poems repeatedly defend the theory and practice of American liberalism, from the anti-Red Scare "Speech for the Repeal of the McCarran Act" to the anti-missile defense "A Fable" (supposedly the only poem Wilbur published in his year under Reagan as the US Poet Laureate). The best of these poems on practical politics remains "For the Student Strikers" (1970), which doubles as worthy advice. "Go talk with those who are rumored to be unlike you", Wilbur advises his pupils:

> Doors will be shut in your faces, I do not doubt.
> Yet here or there, it may be, there will start,
> Much as the lights blink on in a block at evening,
> Changes of heart.

> They are your houses; the people are not unlike you;
> Talk with them, then, and let it be done
> Even for the grey wife of your nightmare sheriff
> And the guardsman's son.

The poems take not just topical positions, but deeper ethical ones to match. Over and over they remind us that nobody has all the answers, that people will hate and kill unless they agree to disagree: "The Undead" even portrays "extremists" as vampires, "Preferring their dreams . . . To the world with all its breakable toys", and "fearing contagion of the mortal". Like Hannah Arendt, or John Stuart Mill for that matter, Wilbur reminds us that the world is far more various, and far less organized, than any one representation, any single idea of the good life, or any one work of art, can represent. "The use of strict poetic forms", Wilbur wrote in 1950, can "serve to limit the work of art, and to declare its artificiality; they say, 'This is not the world, but a pattern imposed upon the world or found in it; this is a partial and provisional attempt.'"

Wilbur's careful stanzas, "blessed by doubt", therefore delight in checks and balances. Sometimes they declare that they have nothing to declare, and always they present their care as a rebuke to confident fanatics, in poetry, governance, cuisine or anything else. Such rebukes even prompt parables. In "A Wood", dominant oaks discover dogwoods and witch hazels, learning that they're not the only beauties under the sun:

> Given a source of light so far away
> That nothing, short or tall, comes very near it,
> Would it not take a proper fool to say
> That any tree has not the proper spirit?
> Air, water, earth and fire are to be blended,
> But no one style, I think, is recommended.

Note that "I think", delighting in doubt within doubt; note the hint of pleasure in its tone.

Wilbur can apparently wield all the rhymed or metred forms the language offers; it would be a shame if he could use them only for subjects of his own devising. Fortunately almost all his books include translations – from Spanish, Russian, French, Italian, Bulgarian; almost all the translations show the polish and thoughtfulness of his original work. Wilbur's Brodsky-in-English sounds better than Brodsky's Brodsky; familiar French poems sound fine, if still familiar (Baudelaire, Villon). The real gems are less well known poets, such as the Bulgarian Valeri Petrov, who let Wilbur try attitudes he might not otherwise attempt, from Petrov's nearly flippant complaint about his advancing age, to Vincius de Moraes' scary cradle song: the latter contrasts the poet's infant daughter with

> The firstborn child within me,
> That cold, petrific, dry
> Daughter whom death once gave,
> Whose life is a long cry
> For milk she may not have.

The last Wilbur – not the most complex, but the most moving – informs certain translations (like the Moraes), certain public poems (say, "Advice to a Prophet") and many pastoral lyrics, then comes into his own in the most recent work. This Wilbur writes quiet poems of memory, elegy, human diminishment and the passing of time. At his best he reminds me of Larkin and Hardy (and of the perpetually-underrated Peter Scupham, the living poet whom Wilbur most resembles). It takes a while to find this sad, personal tone amid the greenery and burnish of Wilbur's earlier work, and most readers seem not to have found it yet. But follow the recollections of childhood, or the accumulation of poems about branches losing their foliage, and there he is – in "Alatus", say, when, "Their supply-lines cut, / The trees go down to defeat". Here he is in animatedly mimetic blank verse from Mayflies (2001), recalling a night drive with his mother and father: "Wild, lashing snow which thumps against the windshield / Like earth tossed down upon a coffin-lid, / Half clogs the wipers, and our Buick yaws / On the black roads of 1928."

And here he is in "Crow's Nests" (also from *Mayflies*), with an extended metaphor, and a pun (on ships' lookouts and carrion crows), which ought to outlive him, and you, and me:

> That lofty stand of trees beyond the field,
> Which in the storms of summer stood revealed
>
> As a great fleet of galleons bound our way
> Across a moiled expanse of tossing hay,
>
> Full-rigged and swift, and to the topmost sail
> Taking their fill and pleasure of the gale,
>
> Now, in this leafless time, are ships no more,
> Though it would not be hard to take them for
>
> A roadstead full of naked mast and spar
> In which we see now where the crow's nests are.

STEPHEN BURT

Watch me skip without your rope

Jack Mapanje, *The Last of the Sweet Bananas: New and Selected Poems*
Bloodaxe Books in association with The Wordsworth Trust,
£9.95, ISBN 1852246650

Oftentimes a poet whose early work is tagged with the label "political" – especially if he is subsequently imprisoned as a consequence – has a hard job escaping that designation throughout his career, no matter which direction his poetry may take. So, while there are several new poems in *The Last of the Sweet Bananas* which suggest he may want to focus on other concerns and other aspects of his life, this may well be the fate of Jack Mapanje, perhaps the most high profile contemporary African poet writing in English. Edgy and engaged as it has always been, Mapanje's poetry never espoused an overt revolutionary agenda or any simple oppositional party line. Rather, like many other African poets writing in English (still the language of power in much of post-colonial Africa), Mapanje has – as he tells us in the introduction to this volume – always felt himself bound to take on the role of "the spokesperson for the so-called 'dregs of society'", a dangerous role to play under a repressive and elitist dictatorship. A radical young intellectual in Hastings Banda's ossifying Malawi, Mapanje was always conscious of the real danger and likely consequences of offending those in power. So he understood the need to write in some sort of code, early poems that appeared uncontroversial – like "Song of Chicken" in the "Cycles" sequence – perhaps bearing a subversive meaning for those with the wit to see through the verbal camouflage:

> Master, you talked with bows,
> Arrows and catapults once
> Your hands steaming with hawk blood
> To protect your chicken.
>
> Why do you talk with knives now,
> Your hands teeming with eggshells
> And hot blood from your own chicken?
> Is it to impress your visitors?

It was appropriate, then, that the teasing, inscrutable chameleon should become the image presiding over Mapanje's early poetry, work rooted in the landscapes and manscapes of Malawi, its history and its traditions, but also looking forward to the emergence of a different kind of society, a democratic meritocracy that might replace the prevailing "political, social and cultural structures that imprison the human spirit and erase creative endeavour and energy". Like so much African literature in English, this is work committed to the notion of poetry as a kind of interventionist social commentary, a poetry of satire and irony intended to expose hypocrisy and undermine the pomposity of those in power. All the same, it is hard to see how it could represent any real threat to an entrenched and all powerful regime like that which Banda had established in Malawi by the mid-1980s. That those in power reacted so brutally to a handful of – seemingly – critical poems tells us much about their insecurity as well as their values.

As was clear from his recent discussion on *Desert Island Discs*, it's not clear, even now, that Jack Mapanje really knows who he had offended or why the response to his first major collection of poems, *Of Chameleons and Gods* should lead first to the book being banned in Malawi, and then to his arrest and imprisonment for almost four years in the notorious Mikuyu Prison in Zomba. The cruelties and injustices of that period of imprisonment haunt Mapanje's imagination still, fifteen years after his release and settled as he is on another continent. The two collections he has published since the Banda regime released him into exile in the UK, have both been dominated by a writing out of the demons of that prison experience. He has spoken and written movingly of the discomfort and distress – although the words are hardly strong enough – of the day-to-day routine in the prison, the ritual humiliations and blatant contempt of Hastings Banda's regime for issues of justice or human rights. "The Streak-Tease At Mikuyu Prison, 25 Sept. 1987", describing his strip-search induction into the prison regime on the night of his arrest is characteristically wry, beginning in a post-grad student memory of "the

striptease at The Bird's Nest / London Street, Paddington in the seventies", and ending with the cruel realisation of his new reality:

> Now the stinking shit-bucket tripped over drowns
>
> The news about the lights being left over night for
> You to scare night creepers, as the putrid bwezi
>
> Blanket-rag enters the single cell & staggers on to
> The cracked cold cement floor of Mikuyu Prison.

That poem is included in the first collection Mapanje published after his release, *The Chattering Wagtails of Mikuyu Prison* (1993), a book which bristles with indignation and outrage, but also retains an ability to laugh at the grim farce that was life inside the prison, and at the ridiculousness of the regime's self-aggrandising pomposities. The spirit of resistance bound up in that mocking laughter is explored in greater depth in the next collection Mapanje published, *Skipping Without Ropes* (1998). The brilliant title poem is a powerful declaration of that human spirit of resistance and of the poet's resilience when confronted by the regime's cruelty and weasel words. Denied skipping ropes to exercise with on the grounds that he might try to harm himself, the poet rhymes "rope" with "hope" to generate a skipping aide as he defies this latest attempt to break his spirit:

> Watch, watch me skip without your
> Rope; watch me skip with my hope –
> a-one, a-two, a-three, a-four, a-five
> I will, a-seven, I do, will skip, a-ten
>
> Eleven, I will skip without, will skip
> Within and skip I do without your
> rope but with my hope; and I will,
> Will always skip you dull, will skip
>
> Your silly rules, skip your filthy walls

Like that imagined rope, the real thing that distinguishes Mapanje's work from the political and prison verse of many other African writers is his apparent belief in – and understanding of – the ways *poetry* works. This is not the by now familiar poetry of statement and protest, simply reflecting back the horror of injustice, cruelty or oppression – shocking and worthy as some of that writing can be. Such work dates and very quickly becomes more interesting to the historian and social scientist than to readers of poetry. Mapanje's measured and crafted poems depend for their authority and their most memorable effects on metaphor and literary cunning. These poems speak far beyond the immediate context of the grim events that inspired their making.

STEWART BROWN

The fragments whole again

Eva Salzman, *Double Crossing New and Selected Poems,*
Bloodaxe, £8.95, ISBN 1852246618

Double Crossing draws on four previous collections, *The English Earthquake* (1992), *Bargain with the Watchman* (1997), *One Two* (2002), and *One Two II* (2003); there are also about three dozen various new poems, mostly in the first section of this volume, "Jesus". There is a recurrent theme of identity, for instance in the poems in "Helen's Sister", which explore doubles and lost halves (the author is a twin), and those in "Homesteading", which reflect her American origins.

More than one recent poem shows an interest in chaos, including "The Lost Mushrooms of Bologna", a sort of hymn to chaos theory. In poems such as this a tendency to agglomerate inessential detail is successful, as it underpins the theme, but elsewhere poems can seem cluttered. They may be rapid but they don't necessarily get to the quick. At the end of "The Buddhas of Bamiyan", for instance, the beautiful notion that it is anti-Buddhist to cling too hard to the giant Afghan icons notoriously blown up by the Taliban, as it denies them their nirvana, is rapidly implied rather than drawn boldly to the surface. The statues, the poem concludes, can still embrace those who would rather die than keep

> each Buddha from divinity: its vanishing trick.
> You who have a mind to, who can think as loftily
> as the Buddhas of Bamiyan, can miss them but let them go.
> Imagine all the fragments whole again,
> and our signature on the empty sky.

This over-rapidity of expression is frustrating partly because Salzman can time excellently: there are good epigrammatic piths in, for example, "Midtown Muzak", about an anti-war march in New York in February 2003:

> The king's bad-ass and big-time troops
> are galloping out of your small-time reach.

There are many excellent endings, too, as in "The Letters I Never Sent" ("What commander is without her past?") or "Forcing Flowers":

> Leaning over, the erstwhile hero
> delicately sniffs: memory *is* a rose.
> Now, we keep hothouses. In them everything stinks.

Salzman's best and most satisfying poems are mostly found towards the back of this volume, from *Bargain with the Watchman*. Here the poems can slow and become reflective. In a poem such as "Cross Out", about girls escaping their parents' house at night to meet boys, the terms are open enough to be the meeting-point for many people's experiences, an uncluttered common territory:

> They must have known that we escaped – if only
> by some slight shade across their dreams –
> how our cunningly angled steps bluffed the old staircase
> from its customary whinge.

Or, from "Pilgrim":

> The beach was a shrine of steel in summer.
> Its muscular heat stunned me face-down in prayer.

A phrase such as "muscular heat" is clean, refers to the sexuality of the beach's inhabitants as well as the sun, and embodies a certain force in the way those stressed first and last syllables hold down the middle two.

Nevertheless, there is often in these poems a residue of compelling opacity: matters are not always easily resolved. The end of "The Pine Barrens" is mysterious and admirably compact:

> Fall empties me, and I sinned by loving
> emptiness, the god-like powers
> of imagining, and god-like pain.

In spring again, in Christian lands
I think: one son's one more than none.
It seems impossible each time, nothing

will come of this – unholy even –
or ever will, you say in bed

one day; I blow my smoke into the air.

The multivalency of the word "Fall" is arresting: it is a religious fall and
possibly a miscarriage, as well as the season. The tortuous syntax for the
tortuous emotion, the marriage of religious register with the image of an
infertile woman smoking on the bed, are deft. There is copious warmth and
invention in Eva Salzman's best work.

KIERON WINN

Fellow democrats

Just the Thing: Selected Letters of James Schuyler 1951–1991
Edited by William Corbett, Turtle Point Press, $21.95, ISBN 1885586302
John Ashbery: Selected Prose
Edited by Eugene Richie, Carcanet Press, £14.95, ISBN 1857547578

In 1970, James Schuyler wrote to Kenward Elmslie on the question of
speaking one's mind: "Do you think one's ego remains intact – in so far as
it does – largely through the courtesy of one's friends?" Less than a year
later, Schuyler suffered the first of what were to be several mental breakdowns
that decade. His friends did what they could to help; a trust was eventually
established to finance his rent and employ an assistant. In the 1970s and 80s,
it was the kindness of friends that Schuyler relied upon – and in turn, *Just the
Thing: Selected Letters of James Schuyler* provides an account of the myriad
courtesies Schuyler extended to (and received from) his friends, some of the
most prominent painters and poets in New York at the time. Schuyler was a
marvellous letter writer, but that conclusion ought not to surprise us. His
poems were often stylistically epistolary. It's one of the sadder ironies that
Schuyler is often depicted as being disengaged from life (often in comparison
with other members of the so-called New York School of Poetry), given that
his writing indicates a huge engagement with and investment in a shared life
with his friends. In this sense, it is somewhat misleading to begin this review

with an account of Schuyler's mental illness because, aside from a few distressingly manic letters, there is very little in this collection to do with his health. His eye is firmly fixed on his friends – their loves, their gossip and their careers. His letters do not always have the ruminative clarity of his diary or poems, but they firmly identify Schuyler as a wit:

> Ah: Lorraine Ellison is singing my top fave of all her numbers on Stay With Me. "Heart Be Still." "HOW! CAN ah FO-get you! How Can Ah Go to SLEEP – oh heart be still – When AH KNOW that AH love YOU?" Great.

Writing to Ashbery, Schuyler gave his assessment of Paganini's *Caprices*: "...half Kilkenny cat & half barbwire; listening to them straight through is as shattering as a box of chocolates with stone centers. Can't wait to play it for you." The book is packed with *bon mots* like these. The collection is just the thing to provide an alternative history of the New York art and poetry world and William Corbett provides a very good introduction; one could only wish for more from him. The book's only problem is the lack of an index.

The danger of gathering together John Ashbery's literary criticism (including, here, fragments of an abandoned doctoral dissertation) is that it might be presented in the name of canonical comprehensiveness. If John Ashbery's *Selected Prose* deserves this criticism more than *Just the Thing*, it is not due to the standard of Ashbery's writing, but because the book was bound to take on a diffuse cast, as it collects together book reviews, introductions to poets' readings and artists' catalogues, addresses to various academic audiences, obituaries, doctoral essays and film reviews. The editor needed to make a clear case to justify this book's publication – but it is debatable whether Eugene Richie succeeds in this task. Furthermore, the articles are placed in chronological order so that (according to Richie), the reader may draw parallels between Ashbery's poetry and prose – but there are few editorial footnotes to kick-start this kind of critical echo sounding. As a result, the book has a supplementary rather than necessary air.

This is a shame, because many of the reviews and articles anthologised here are fantastic (see, for example, the articles on Robert Mapplethorpe and Joe Brainard). Though most were written to support a poetry career, and not to provide a possible thematic index to his poetry, they survive the transition well. There is a surprising degree of aesthetic continuity. Ashbery has always championed writers and artists who showed little interest in paying allegiance to wider artistic movements or who worked without critical acclaim. This collection merely establishes this trend more firmly. It is made quite clear (in several articles) that he thought the French Surrealist practice of automatic writing dubious. There are only two film reviews in the book, but both films delight Ashbery in very similar ways. He likes the way that the amassing of tiny details in a work produces its own creative power, how the piling up of seemingly inconsequential detail causes the viewer to be "so aware of the passage of time that a trivial piece of action can have the force of a pistol shot". Comments like these can easily operate as summaries of what is good about Ashbery's own poetry. It is also clear that his ability as a critic derives in part from his talent for analogy. Marianne Moore's poems start "like a ride on a roller coaster, smoothly and calmly enough, and in no time at all one is clutching the bar with both hands". The moments of sudden clarity in Gertrude Stein's writing are experienced "as though a change in the wind had suddenly enabled us to hear a conversation that was taking place some distance away".

James Schuyler's *Selected Letters* and John Ashbery's *Selected Prose* were bound to illuminate each other – Schuyler and Ashbery were close friends from 1951, worked as art critics and edited a literary magazine together, and even co-wrote a novel. According to Schuyler, Ashbery was one of the great correspondents in his life (the other was Joe Brainard). Commenting on Ashbery's influence on his poetry, he noted, "It has a great deal to do with John's sensibility, his terrific taste. He really has great taste. He can sort of make taste a matter of ethics". *Selected Prose* goes a long way to proving Schuyler's point, and *Just the Thing* demonstrates just how Ashbery's enthusiasms were reciprocated in kind by Schuyler:

> Fellow Democrat;
>
> Your last letter – what a joy. Naturally I couldn't answer it immediately, I was bent too double with mirth, and the only thing that straightened me up was your searingly intelligent and lovely review in *Poetry*. As Furl said, "It's so – CLEAR. You can see all the way around to a – 180 DEGREE ANGLE." Fairfield [Porter]'s world, you see, is really only half a world; I liked it because I could see all the way around 359 degrees where I found Kim Novak smiling on the last degree.

The review Ashbery had written was of Gertrude Stein's *Stanzas in Meditation* (included in *Selected Prose*), in which, as William Corbett notes, Ashbery had indeed managed the unlikely feat of mentioning Novak (star of film biography *Jeanne Eagles*). In these two books then, the reader is presented with panoramic views of culturescapes in the late twentieth-century – to find Ashbery and Schuyler smiling (sometimes at each other) on the last degree.

JENNI QUILTER

Accessibility: a Catullus for now?

Catullus: Poems of Love and Hate, translated by Josephine Balmer,
Bloodaxe, £7.95, ISBN 1852246456

"One of the main purposes of education is to encourage people to think. But education for its own sake is a bit dodgy" (see http://news.bbc.co.uk/1/hi/education/2712833.stm). These reported comments of former Education Minister Charles Clarke are from January 2003, and were followed up by the observation that, while he did in fact advocate the study of philosophy, he was "less occupied by the Classics". The timing of these remarks, in the run up to the second Gulf War, seems either proof of synchronicity or provides further evidence of myopia as this government peers across its long-range cultural origins and present circumstances without an understanding of either.

On the face of it, there might not be much the Blair government and the world of the late Roman Republic, or the first years of Augustus, have in common, but all the poets of that period seemed to be against war except Virgil (and possibly Horace). Their engagement with the subject now sounds urgent and relevant. Neither Catullus (84–54 BC) nor the later Roman elegists had much time for the pursuit of war or the manipulations of politicians, except as metaphor for love and illicit bedroom activity. Catullus is famous for his excoriations of Caesar, Propertius for his avoidance strategies around dedicating books of poetry to Augustus and his military exploits. Much is made of his use of the rhetorical device the "recusatio", or refusal, to write of wider political and public themes. Tibullus and Ovid are even more overt in their rejections of the soldier's life. Consider Propertius's *Elegies* (II.15):

> If every man wanted to live their life like mine,
> at leisure, arms and legs droopy with wine
> There would be no vicious blades or war galleons,
> Actium's waves would not break on our bones,
> Nor Rome, often victim of her own ambitions
> shy away from proper displays of grief.
> This thing our forebears will grace us with certitude:
> *our* skirmishes never caused gods fury.
> (my translation)

Clarke has also levelled the charge that subjects worthy of study "need a relationship with the workplace". All sorts of questions are raised with this remark. If you want to become a politician, what about Cicero's speeches, or Plato or Aristotle? Where else is the foundation of Western democracy other than in the Ancient worlds of Greece and Rome? Where else would you find the ideological bases of New Labour and the Neo-Cons and the institutions they exist in? So much of contemporary culture is still presented in Graeco-Roman terms, and most negative aspects of empire are latent in this background and history: slavery, the second-class status of women, racism, elitism, jingoism, and nationalism. These concepts, and ways of being and living, start in Greece and Rome for Western democracies, and need to be traced in their terms, before they can be related to our own.

Catullus became the most translated Latin poet in the twentieth century (see *Catullus in English*, Julia Haig Glaisser, Penguin, 2001). This trend has accelerated the translation of other Latin poets of this period in the last fifteen to twenty years. Ovid and Propertius, in particular, have benefited. As study of the Classical languages has decreased over recent years, translations have increased with the popularity of courses in Latin and Greek cultural history. Therefore, if students are to become reliant on English versions of Ancient texts then they should be the best representations of that culture at all levels of translation, from the textual through the contextual to the cultural.

Doubtless Charles Clarke would find much to approve in the new Catullus of Josephine Balmer. If we are going to tolerate the Classics in our ahistorical culture of immediacy, transparency and instant understanding then this is the Catullus for the age of New Labour. Balmer reveals her aesthetic with that watch-word of government education and arts policy: "accessibility". Her principle of translation is based "most importantly, on a desire for the poetry to be as accessible as possible, as enjoyable . . . to those with no prior knowledge of Latin or the poet." Toward this goal, Balmer presents the poems thematically, and gives them titles. She cuts out almost all the long poems, the ones of difficulty, with mythological themes and alien marriage rituals, to leave the epigrams and shorter elegies. This editing exaggerates Catullus's blessing and curse: he seems so fresh, so adolescent, so "now".

But what is wrong with Balmer's approach? Don't the poems become more understandable to an audience of the twenty-first century? They certainly come to resemble the discreet lyric, acceptable as the modern face of English poetry since 1950. However, the 116 poems are in an order already coherent and intelligent, and make sense with a little effort of study. The order could have been concocted in the Renaissance, as Balmer points out, but recent research about papyrus of the late Republican period is compelling. The argument goes that the physical length of the papyrus roll fits perfectly the three groups (or "books") Catullus has made by metre. That the poems should have come down to a modern audience in this way Balmer calls "the second miracle". I believe in that miracle, a chiastic miracle that pivots at the very centre of the book in Poem 64: Theseus' black-sailed boat disappears from Ariadne's gaze and looms on the horizon for Aegeus, his father, without the white sail that would signify Theseus' safe return. The black sail Aegeus sees he misinterprets as a sign of his son's death, and so he throws himself from the cliff-tops. Cutting out long poems like Poem 64 destroy the symmetry and design that is quite other to contemporary ideas of aesthetic order, but absolutely vital and necessary to a clear view of this book and the late Roman Republic.

There is other evidence that corroborates this interpretation. The codex (a way of distributing text that resembles the modern book) was not invented until c.70 AD, a hundred years after Catullus. Martial's epigrams appeared in this form. A change of format changes a book's length, and it seems plausible there would have been texts circulating of this type by Catullus. Or maybe not. We know Catullus had "disappeared" by the second century AD; perhaps this was not only because his style of poetry had become unfashionable, but also because the format in which it was distributed was no longer cutting edge enough for the literati. A bit like carting around a Corona typewriter when everyone else carries an iBook.

Further to this "physical" evidence, Catullan aesthetics are also problematic for Balmer's project. Catullus was part of a group called the neoterics. They based their art on learning, and allusion, and saw their tradition beginning with Alexandrian poets writing in Greek, like Callimachus. Most importantly of all, their aesthetic was based on form, and, I suspect, not just in individual poems but also as design of a whole group or book of poems. Their idea was to wear learning very much on the sleeve, to show-off. And indeed, it is important to realise that Catullus was writing for *literary* friends, and those of a certain class, not anybody like a general reader. Coterie was good not bad. Our idea of accessibility would seem not only alien to Catullus, but hostile to this notion of championing difficulty. The translator of Catullus and academic Charles Martin has likened Catullus and the group around him to the early High Modernists, Eliot, Pound, etc, and it is certainly true that Catullus's aesthetic seemed attractive to Pound, and was an influence on his poetry.

Then, in Balmer, there is the twenty-first-century apparatus: the use of themes and titles as an organisational principle of the collection, which is severely flawed. No Latin poet uses titles for their poems. They (Catullus in particular) would be completely bewildered with this innovation, and would see these signposts as entirely misleading. The ordering by theme harks back to a trend for Catullan translation from the 1930s and 1940s: at best it appears

quaint now. Critically, the ordering of poems by theme starts to break down as we see Poem 45 (using the original "three book" numbering) appear on page 66 with its own section, "IV Love, Requited". One short lyric with its own section? This quirk highlights the weakness of thematic methodology, and reads both awkwardly and lamely.

A more compelling argument, still, against the thematic organisation of poems has to do with repetition. Group all the really great poems together and their repetitions and refrains become boring. These are poems that should be separated by other poems, and opened out with other ideas and preoccupations, not bunched and corralled into themes like sheep. To sort the poems into these groupings misses the vitality of the poet's work. All these poems, on their various topics, reflect a various shape to a very particular life. There are poems about Catullus's affair with Lesbia, poems to friends, to enemies, his criticism of career politicians, poems on myths – all these are part of a rich, precious, detailed and unquantifiable life, a continuum. The strange mix that are the "three books" reflect this life under a discipline of various poetic forms and metres. The ordering of the texts fundamentally determines how we read them in their detail; the entirety matters as much as the minutiae, so Balmer's sound and sometimes terrific translations get buried by this misleading imposition of thematic accessibility.

Poems of Love and Hate crosses the boundary from creative representation to a dangerously twisted caricature of this body of work and the society that bore it. Reducing Catullus's "books" to a thematic structure means we can't see through to the culture of the late-Roman Republic; Josephine Balmer interprets the work of this great Roman poet, moving away from its cultural roots, crushing it into a shape that resembles our own. There is no respect for difference here, and in overturning aesthetic values the cultural ones are obfuscated too. This book, in other words, fulfils all the accessibility criteria whilst failing those of authenticity.

The more one studies Catullus the less his world seems to resemble ours: on that impression many translators, commentators and scholars have agreed. It is an indictment of where we are now, and a weakness of our own literary culture, that a translator of Balmer's capabilities should see these differences homogenised and not cherished.

SIMON SMITH

The bottleneck effect

Anthologies of French poetry and the *fin-de-siècle*

It is a melancholy thing, when reviewing anthologies, to observe the winnowing process at work. This is exacerbated when a whole century of poetry is to be represented in a single volume: the "bottleneck effect" becomes critical. Numerous are the poets of the mid-century, let us say, in anthologies of the mid-century, who have fallen off the perch by the end of it. The anthologist is like some lumbering beast of burden, whose load is unceasingly increased; there is the slippage and settling of transit, and then some precious stuff falls off, and then whole saddlebags go missing as the century advances. If one could be certain that the goods remaining on board are necessarily superior, made of more lasting material than those jettisoned, then the natural dismay one feels at seeing individuals erased would be a little offset. It is not just individuals, but sometimes the whole crowd, a whole anthology that goes missing in these brutal culls of the *fin-de-siècle*. I remember with fondness an influential volume that was ubiquitous when I first visited France, Bernard Delvaille's *Poètes des années soixante* with its hipster denim cover. The Cambridge University library does not appear to hold a copy, and I suspect that not a single representative of that liberated company has survived the massacre. They have moved, or been moved, into outer darkness.

Having recently edited an anthology myself (Faber's *Twentieth-Century French Poems*, 2002), I started browsing, out of curiosity and a certain fellow-feeling, the efforts of my remoter predecessors in this field, and it is this activity that revealed to me the extent of our savagery, which is beyond even what I imagined. But another melancholy truth was simultaneously brought home to me, that the "public at large" was possibly not too concerned that the "towering efforts" of, let us say, Patrice de la Tour du Pin's nine-volume *Somme de Poésie*, recounting in huge elaboration one individual's Spiritual Odyssey, is nowhere to be found in the various end-of-century summaries, including my own. Not a trace of it, not the faintest spoor. Who gives a toss? I say this because, on the evidence of the flyleaf, Paul Auster's still classic bi-lingual *Random House Book of Twentieth-Century French Poetry* (1984), has remained on the stacks these twenty years undisturbed. Unless I am wrong, no one had even opened the book until I borrowed it a few days ago. And that is in the open stacks of a great university library; so if not here . . . then where? My curiosity piqued, I ventured further back. Here is Graham Dunstan Martin's superbly edited Anthology of Contemporary French Poetry,

constituting the fifth volume of the Edinburgh University's "Bilingual Library" (1972). Dunstan Martin's introduction includes a luminous discussion of the perennial quarrel about "a language suitable for poetry" that has always seemed to trouble Gallic heads more than their island neighbours'. Alas, the nuanced argument has been lost on the public, for I have evidence that only one reader has borrowed this book in thirty-two years. A single hit! The ongoing editions (1952–1976) of Cecil Arthur Hackett's pioneering *Anthology of Modern French Poetry* scores five hits spread over three versions of the book, which averages out at around one reader every ten years. The longevity of his excellent edition also allows him to add two new poets – Yves Bonnefoy and André du Bouchet – which is an honour indeed, since they are the end of a line beginning with Baudelaire, Mallarmé and Verlaine . . . . The four or so Cambridge readers since 1976 will have received the benefit of these two judicious additions.

Having caught the catalogue bug now, and full of hope, I looked up an *Anthology of Modern French Poetry* (Senior Course), edited by C. Cassal and T. Karcher. I found it was published in 1876, and went missing in 1888. It is like a blessed break. Perhaps the book was smuggled out of the library by some Swinburnean youth overheated by the *Epaves* of Baudelaire, and made its way in the world, where it may have done some good. Who knows? That addendum – "Senior Course" – is rather a downer, however.

Of course I exaggerate, but not much. Whether they are much read anyway, or not, it is instructive to compare these mid-century anthologies of French poetry destined for an Anglophone readership, in translation and otherwise, with their end-of-century counterparts. It is less the novelties that concern me here, than the forgotten and the dropped. The rejectamenta. In spite of ourselves, and this is true even of the most determinedly and cheerily inclusive *omnium gatherum*, such as Mary Ann Caws's big new brick from Yale, every anthologist is building up a *salon des réfusés*; with each inclusion think how many deserving others are turned away, pale reproachful ghosts that would, were there any justice, prey on the anthologist's mind in the small hours. The mischievous *Zeitgeist* is everywhere at work. Like Lyell's fossils, whole strata seem to have gone missing, life-forms wiped off the record. Most strikingly, and in a way shockingly, the great Catholic tradition that celebrates, in heightened language and with religious rhetoric something comprehensively known as "le sacré", seems to have been suppressed – the word is scarcely too strong. Obliterated in Auster altogether, as belonging "in spirit to an earlier time", this tradition's most unignorable representative, Paul Claudel, is restored in Caws, as is one descendant, Jean Grosjean, but there is no sign now of Patrice de la Tour du Pin, Pierre Emmanuel, or the much younger, grandiloquent successor to Saint-John Perse, Pierre Oster-Soussouev. A slightly older Catholic poet, Jean-Claude Renard (b. 1922) who is a significant presence in Dunstan Martin's 1972 anthology, described by him as "one of France's finest contemporary poets", has simply vanished, and established more centrally in his stead is the celebrated group of his contemporaries that clustered around the review *Epéemère* – Bonnefoy, Dupin, du Bouchet, and Jaccottet. And here it seems that to belong to a "school", however loose or illusory the affiliations really are, is an aid to survival. Think of Macspaunday, or, above all, of the Surrealists.

Since none of these "poetes du sacré", to give them a convenient sobriquet, appear in my anthology either, I feel required to submit myself to an *examen de conscience* or at least explain their exclusion. Writing in 1950 or so, my predecessor C.A.Hackett describes the poetry of Patrice de la Tour du Pin in his judicious way: "*Une Somme de Poésie* attempts to create a poetic and religious myth, an undertaking which, in the present state of our civilization, cannot but be artificial and incoherent…". What, then, has happened to that mammoth effort ("nine books so far published…")? I rescue it from the shelves. I find a poetry of exaltation, of high rhetorical charge, of exclamation, of myth-making; an elaborate and baffling hybrid of poetry, prose and drama, much of it impenetrable on a swift reading. I rescue Pierre Emmanuel's *Le grand oeuvre / cosmogonie* and find apostrophes like: "Pourquoi la Vie? / Pourquoi, Père, as-Tu donné la vie?" Surveying these gigantic abandoned constructs, remote as engines from Nineveh, it appears that a whole language has been sheared away, that high style inspired by the psalmodic verset, championed by Claudel and Saint-John Perse. Their youngest avowed disciple, Pierre Oster-Soussouev (b. 1933), early on declared the poet's main task to be "l'affirmation de l'âme", and dismissed Lautréamont, Rimbaud and Breton as "ces stupides féroces". But on the evidence of these anthologies, it seems that the ferocious fools have comprehensively trounced the opposition. Looking again at Oster's work, its afflatus, or what the French call *souffle*, is extremely off-putting. His habit of titling his poems, portentously, by numbers, "*douzième poeme*", or "*treizième poeme*", is an added irritation. There is undoubtedly, whether explicitly or otherwise, a political dimension to all this. Two centuries of struggle between Church and State have left their clawmark on the poetry. The high Catholic style, with the poets up on stilts, is too redolent of the sacrificial rant of a Maurice Barrès, whose armchair patriotism became so irksome to the *poilus* at the front. It brings bad memories. To the left-leaning Surrealists, and to a poet like Ponge, it was quite simply repellent. If a certain type of poetic diction has become discredited, it is a measure of their influence, and of the extraordinary hold that Breton and Aragon in particular exerted on aesthetic and political questions before and after the Second World War. In a word, like all powerful poets, they effected a comprehensive change in taste.

Perhaps the ideal anthologist is precisely the one who should therefore rescue the discredited, and allow the lesser voices to sound, give room to those on the margins and above all remember the lone wolves and the solitaries. But the anthologist is as subject to changes in taste as anyone else. Part of his or her job is to indicate where the most vital work is to be found. I would give all of Oster's or Pierre Emmanuel's apostrophes to the Light or to the Earth, for Apollinaire's "vieille paire de chaussures jaunes devant la fenêtre", those yellow shoes glimpsed and immortalized in his simultaneist poem "Les Fenêtres". Likewise, Reverdy's lamp seen through a window, or Ponge's humble fruit crate, or Jean Follain's red apple or hardware store. These poets have set themselves the more modest, and more difficult, task of rescuing the humble object and the fleeting moment, *et sans commentaire*. There is a line that runs from Apollinaire, Reverdy, Fargue and Follain, down through Philippe Jaccottet, Jacques Réda, Guy Goffette, Paul de Roux and Gilles Ortlieb which constitutes, for me, one of the most vital and interesting in French poetry of the last century, and alongside the great "unavoidables", in my own anthology I have tried to highlight it. It is as far from the afflatus of an Oster as it is from that brand of post-Mallarméan minimalism that spread like a virus during the years of high structuralism and *Tel Quel*.

That is my particular preference. Paul Auster gives more space to minimalism and radical experimentation, Mary Ann Caws to the OuLiPo and Lettriste poets and their descendants, like Jacques Roubaud, Michelle Grangaud, Emmanuel Hocquard, and the busy duo Pierre Alféri and Olivier Cadiot (who is translated in her book by Charles Bernstein, thereby "flagging" another Franco-American affiliation, which is a significant chapter in the history of both poetries in the last century). Caws has also dramatically turned the volume up for women. The statistics here are telling: Auster includes only one, Anne-Marie Albiach, I include seven, and Caws thirty-one. For contemporary women poets she has also drawn on the excellent work of Martin Sorrell and his volume *Elles* (Exeter, 1995). There is no question that in terms of sheer inclusiveness – Caws has 120 poets, compared to Auster's 48 and my own haul of 54 in the Faber anthology – she has comprehensively overhauled her predecessors. She sets out quite clearly her criteria: "My commitment is to a wide reach of works, with all the risk that entails, and to the judgement of the translators I have called upon…". She is careful to include poets of the wider reaches of the Francophone community, poets of négritude and their successors, and poets of the Quebecois constituency (which includes one of the best poets of all, Anne Hébert). Disarmingly, she owns up to risks and gambles, and acknowledges the relatively small number of poems allotted to each poet – in many cases poets are represented by only one. It is here she falls down badly compared to Auster. But her own energy is titanic and deserves to be saluted. She herself has translated hundreds of poems in the anthology, far more than anybody else. She provides a general introduction, and mini-presentations of each poet represented, as well as a short introductions to each section. The result is a rich, cacophonous, and at times vexing book. But that is the nature of the beast, a whole century of poetry from France, Africa, Canada and elsewhere; it is multitudinous, protean, and obviously utterly ungraspable in any univocal way. *The Yale Anthology of Twentieth Century French Poetry* contains a fair sampling of it, and that is already to say a lot. But as I have tried to show, even such a capacious volume as this is not by any means the whole story.

STEPHEN ROMER

Anthologies referred to:

The Yale Anthology of Twentieth-Century French Poetry, ed. Mary Ann Caws, Yale University Press, 2004
Twentieth-Century French Poems, ed. Stephen Romer, Faber, 2002
The Random House Book of Twentieth Century French Poetry, ed. Paul Auster, Vintage, 1984
Anthology of Contemporary French Poetry, ed. Graham Dunstan Martin, Edinburgh Bilingual Library (5), University of Edinburgh, 1972
Anthology of Modern French Poetry, ed C.A. Hackett, Blackwell, 1952 (and subsequent editions)
New French Poetry, ed. C.A. Hackett, Blackwell, 1973
Elles, ed. Martin Sorrell, University of Exeter, 1995

A butcher thinks about sex

Sean Cole, *Itty City*, Pressed Wafer, $5, ISBN 0972108999
Jack Evans, *Work*, Pressed Wafer, $5, ISBN 097210898X
Mark Lamoureux, *29 Cheeseburgers*, Pressed Wafer, $5, ISBN 0972108971
Joseph Torra, *After the Chinese*, Pressed Wafer, $12, ISBN 0975323709

In a recent lecture, Don Paterson offered a personal definition of poetry thus: "a poem is just a little machine for remembering itself". Although these four American poets reflect the entire spectrum of poetic practice, from the immediately accessible to the deliberately opaque, all four seem to challenge that definition. They are memorable writers; but the reader, on returning to the work, will not encounter a set of pre-programmed emotive triggers, nor a perfect mnemonic corroboration. As in Heraclitus's much-quoted aphorism – that you cannot step into the same river twice – these poems cannot be read identically from one encounter to the next. Or, as Sean Cole writes, rather more elegantly, in "Daimler-Chrysler":

> I write this as I listen to the radio. I'm a difficult person to know, I hear.
> Any controversial proposition is dual. (I came away from this poem, had dinner
> and came back, stayed in the house) . . . .
> 　　　　　　　　　Come in! I'm writing two different poems this moment,
> One's finished. Thus so is the other!

Jack Evans's poetry offers, on the surface, few difficulties. *Work* consists of dramatic monologues and short lyrics on the theme of employment. The "story" aspects are handled with consummate concision, especially in "A Ride With The Dying Man", where a cab driver picks up a man "pale as a toadstool". To counteract the effects of emphysema, he knows the exact speed that, with the windows down, will simulate normal breathing. It's worthy of Carver at his best. Its poetic aspects are subtle: ulterior meanings in "labored" breath, an ambiguous "tip". When he says "you did a good job", it's unclear whether he's referring to the mere service or a more tenuous act of sympathy. The hidden human values of workplace relations structure the collection, most effectively in "Barnyard", where a butcher thinks about sex, a lamb thinks about its mother, and "The knife / thinks // only / of itself".

Imitations of Chinese poetry can be as gloopy as sweet-and-sour-cook-in-sauce; it is therefore a pleasant discovery to find in Joseph Torra's collection a more mature and sophisticated homage. Rather than the willow-pattern caricatures of reeds and bridges, the world of these poems is pressingly modern: it's against "Money. Power. Position" that the words unfurl. Torra deploys broad and biting humour reminiscent of Chih-Kuei as an antidote to the lotus-gazing, as in "Attend reading / without a measly / ten bucks to buy / the poet's book". It is, however, the last section, "The Golden Notebook of Love", which is the most nuanced. It is a long meditation on romantic loss, where even "the days long". As much as he tries to "look / for words that bind / us both", the assertion of love becomes a memory of loss.

29 Cheeseburgers is a more complex volume. Like a more calorific Proustian madeleine, these "edged circle[s] of nausea" conjure various losses. Lamoureux has a quiet but convincing surrealism; as he says "whenever tragedy smacks / I think of smiling elves". The poetry reflects the "constant crush of tongues" in the modern city: Japanese cartoons and bureaucratic jargon, advertising jingles and ouija board jinks. It's an interzone, where you "can't tell the cafes from the bars". Cutting through the white noise is a powerfully articulated vision of complex emotions; a simultaneous blending of cynicism and hopefulness. "Would that I were / punk rock & could / care less about those girls". Evoking, as in Torra, also involves admitting absence.

Finally, Sean Cole's deeply weird, but magnificently entertaining, *Itty City*. The book has an energy partly derived from Frank O'Hara's jazz-like improvisation, partly parodying hip-hop flyting. "Letter to Self, Found in Powder-Filled Envelope" opens "We know what 'haver' means you incessant poet", and goes on to berate the author's supposed obscurity: "Your dark apothegms don't faze me". Playfulness patters throughout the book, with Cole inventing dates (Kleptember 5th, Imbroglio the 29th), and manically rewriting submission letters to poetry journals. This resists synopsis to the utmost degree: perhaps the only way to convey its unique flavour, remarkable skill and political edge is to quote one work in full, "Alphabet Poem":

> Zorba, you xenophobe. Will vaunted
> uglyisms triumph? Stay recent. Quit
> preaching old nomenclature.
> Maybe labelling Kurds "jerks" isn't
> helping. Greet foes equally.
> Despotism could bring
> Armageddon.

Memorable, certainly. But, as Cole understands, old words carry old grievances.

STUART KELLY

Poet in the Gallery

WILLIAM CORBETT

Jane Freilicher, *Paintings, 1954–2004*
Tibor de Nagy Gallery, New York, New York
Jane Freilicher, by Klauss Kertess,
Harry N. Abrams, Inc, Publishers, $60, ISBN 0810949636

This mini-retrospective celebrated the publication of *Jane Freilicher*, a coffee table book with text by Klaus Kertess and essays by John Ashbery and the painter Thomas Nozkowski. The exhibition confirmed what has been known for some time, that Freilicher is a marvelous painter, one of the best of her generation – a fact now documented between hard covers for all to see.

In its meandering, out of focus, and, at times, sloppy way Kertess outlines Freilicher's career. (She deserves better and gets it from Ashbery and Nozkowski.) Ketress plays close attention to her friendship with her contemporaries Ashbery, Barbara Guest, Kenneth Koch, Frank O'Hara and James Schuyler, the first generation of the New York School of Poets. The book begins with Schuyler's poem "Looking Forward to Seeing Jane Real Soon", thus homing in on Freilicher's true aesthetic soul-mate among her poet friends. Like Schuyler's poems, Freilicher's paintings are straightforward, intimate, lucid and, at their core, serene – she is the muse of serenity. In their off-hand way they command assent, a yes that is agreement, admiration and something deeper. Theirs is art that embodies, in Schuyler's words, "the world in its impurity which is so very beautiful and acceptable, if only because one has so little choice".

Kertess agrees with the familiar line that Freilicher's work grew from her studies with Hans Hoffman, the abstract painting in fashion during her youth, and the impact on her of Bonnard – to whose work she was exposed at the influential 1948 exhibition at MOMA – and Vuillard. What sets her work apart from her masters is air and light. Where Bonnard and Vuillard seem mostly to have looked in, and where even Bonnard's outdoors seems interior, Freilicher, in her downtown studio or Long Island home, looks out. She is a painter of afternoon and evening light. The world outside her ostensible subject, the cut flowers she loves to paint, is in her pictures. Another way to see this is that the subjects of so many of her pictures are seen in the world from which they come.

What's missing in this big book, as always in reproductions, is the paint

> The buildings seen are close together like those in a Tuscan hilltop village. In the distance rise four Con-Edison smokestacks, and beyond their smoke the evening sky turns pink.

itself. At Tibor de Nagy you could trace Freilicher's surfaces from her early, thickly brushed strokes on loan from the abstract painting then ruling downtown New York, to the opened-up sketch-like casual blending, the abstract figuration, of her early 1960s Long Island landscapes. Her stroke tightened in a series of chaste nudes in the late 1960s, and from then through to the present her surfaces look effortless and feel lived in. There is no striving after effect, nor is there a feeling of working within limits. She is painting exactly as she wants, in that zone where thought and act are one.

Since the late 1960s she has put vases, often non-descript containers like jars and cups, before windows looking out on an eastern Long Island landscape or downtown New York City. The beautifully plain song to New York, "Early New York Evening" (1954), in both exhibition and book, shows that this view was in her eye from the start. Blue irises, the common variety, stand in a green vase before the view of lower Manhattan Freilicher saw from the studio on East 11th Street that she sublet for $11.35 a month. The buildings seen are close together like those in a Tuscan hilltop village. In the distance rise four Con-Edison smokestacks, and beyond their smoke the evening sky turns pink. The painting communicates comfort, nostalgia, or whatever that yearning for what one has is called, and contemplation, a looking out that becomes looking in. What is elegiac in the painting recalls the last line of Schuyler's immaculate "view" poem "February", "it is a day like any other." Unremarkable like all but a handful of days, until remarked on in paint.

Over the next fifty years Freilicher refines this view and extends what it takes in. On Long Island the light is early afternoon, the flowers gathered and arranged, it seems, by the painter. Just what gives her pleasure to look at and paint. The summer outdoors hums in contentment. (In the 1980s she begins to focus on the landscape in summer and in a few frosty, invigorating winter scenes.) In New York City she often paints dusk – chrome pink, fire reflected and softened – a time she owns.

These are signature arrangements and moments, fresh almost every time she returns to them – her vision is no less strong for appearing relaxed – but there are other Freilicher's that stand out and apart. "Still Life with Calendulas" (1955), at 651/2" x 49 1/2" a big painting for her, is a studio arrangement of flowers in a blue and white vase among the folds of a hanging flowered curtain. For me it is the painting in which Freilicher takes what she needs from her French ancestors, their understanding of the expressive power of décor, and moves on. It is as bold as it has to be. "At Night" (1997), commented on by Ashbery, is Spartan in its alignment on a yellow table of a green medicine bottle, waxen leaved plant in terra cotta planter sitting on a glass brick, and blue pottery jug. Ashbery finds "something almost frightening" in the painting. Perhaps it is the fierce attention these objects command. Mere looking is not enough. The objects are implacable, confident, but intense in their demand. The night beyond is murky. A similar painting is "Goldenrod" (1999). A field of goldenrod is seen in detailed fronds in the foreground, a frowsy yellow in mid-distance, and beyond it the water of a pond and the distant flat, tree-filled landscape. Like "At Night" nothing happens in this painting, and yet I want to look at both of them for a long time. The claim on our attention is powerful precisely because it is understated. This is not "Take it or leave it" but "Here it is if you want it"; which is exactly the way the world presents itself for our baffled pleasure and wonderment.

For me this is summed up in a painting that looks nothing like a summation of anything. It is "The Painting Table" (1954); a painting owned by Ashbery and reproduced on the cover of his collected art criticism *Reported Sightings*. An open window shows that outside it is night. The table cluttered with the tools of the trade – upright brushes in jars, tubes of oil paint, charcoal sticks, tins of varnish all without their names drawn on – and at the front of the table the painter's palette is done for the day. The painter's gaze, and the viewer's as well, is affectionate. Out of these utensils has come the painting we see, and what we see is a tribute to them and, in my view, to painting itself. The wonder of it is that one, what is on the table, becomes the other, the painting. The mystery of this alchemy is not diluted by its being obvious.

In Schuyler's poem "Looking Forward to seeing Jane Real Soon", the world in its months, skies, colors and seasons, puts on a show: "And it was all for her." Perhaps this is where the calm in Freilicher's work originates, in her intuiting and welcoming what is hers. Wherever this serenity springs from, it feels like balm, the world looked at for itself without the human tension of feeling one must do something, or anything, with it but look unabashedly – the world all for you.

Answers to the Poetry Review Crossword No. 6:
Across: 6 Faber and Faber, 8 Salt, 9 Enitharmon, 10 U-Bend, 11 Hafnium, 15 Arc, 16 Salvoes, 17 Pap, 20 Spinels, 21 Casca, 24 Hearing eye, 26 Minx, 27 Reality Street. **Down:** 1 Abating, 2 Creel, 3 Anti, 4 Offhanded, 5 Brook, 6 Flambard, 7 Barque, 12 Anvil, 13 D'Annunzio, 14 Carcanet, 18 Sparta, 19 Malmsey, 22 Jeers, 23 Yeats, 25 Enya. **Winner:** Susan Woodman

National Poetry Competition

The first, second and third prize-winners in the National Poetry Competition 2004 are listed below. Prizes totalled £6,500 in cash, plus publication of the winning poems in *Poetry Review*. The judges were Ciaran Carson, Elaine Feinstein, Simon Smith and Denis MacShane (Chair).

First Prize

Jon Sait

HOMELAND

them come at midnight i remember that
i was fooding the cat
      what happened to the cat
in and across the hall them was
before the last bod slam the door
i was scared more for décor
all bootmark in the twill
mud set to stone too quick in nape and alley
and fuss would follow
      anyway
them wanted to know why it was off
i often have it off i said which made them laff
all bellyjig and straining like at shit
then them poke me one with a stick and ask again
not ask exact more shout and kick
i sleep deep and dream i said upstanding
and has no need of it
all flattering from dull mouth or some sunny play
      gobbing did it good for me then
hit me and down i was
with stompers flying in all crowblack and beaky
i pass over then and only come to when rain wet me
it was chillstone and the dark was eyeless
and all was lone and bleedy

> three days least them probe me
all think sore and head reely
then the white light
the bright light
the light like light that change it ever

illuminati

them let me go then after fingering
and promise to never do
now i venge in the not quite dark
all flicker flash and wheezy
i leave the sash open so the whole street can see me
and them that watch can think me safely home

Second Prize
Matthew Caley

L.Z

> Apparently born of a hinny and her ass
> he hee-haws awesomely: of the little words and letters
> like 'A' and 'and' and 'as', and yet – alas, alack –
> never saw the major work complete; of sawhorses
> strung with lanterns in a Brooklyn
> Street – wherein two 'A's made the 'M' of the Latin word 'manes'
> and therein made their manes; inverted they made 'W' for 'Will' – The Bard
> [he pondered, exclusively on his *Bottom*]; of the city that never sleeps
> – of whom another dared to think a geodesic dome, *a la mode,*

over New York like an atmosphere solidified –

that never sleeps except for the zed-zed-zeds of the fire-escapes;

of barely scraping his room and board

to light the low gas-flame or the 'live flame

of tradition' wherein they brook no line

that doesn't sing as such: '*If seahorses*

could but sing Offenbach, Father' – alas-alack –

of a man who for forty-six years watered a single letter, yet was

left with nothing but the odour of odourless zinnias.

Third Prize
Mario Petrucci
GENE

With pollution and GM, future seas may change colour.

Worl alway same   me rekon
nuttin much-change   Dere alway green
melon-anana   Alway yelow-sea

Me granee she live-be twennysix
wit ray hair   Me tel me-babee
we not die-soon   We like granee –

we live-long   An me caree-she
for look-see thru eave – for look
yelow-sea   An me tel-she

wen de-Life tek-you you com
yelow like you fall-in yelow-sea   An
you stopp   Dat all

An me tel-she bout ol-peepol
hoo-liv wen Worl dri   Me tel-she
storee bout way ting used-be

wen ol-peepol walk in air an walk
wid weel   An way dem ol-peepol talk
in riddl   An way dem stepp in someting

dey call   Gene   Yeh   Dem mess-up
reel-bad someting call Gene   An dem
rising-now for meet-us in yelow-sea

An me-babee say – *Dees storee*
all troo? Dem ol-peepol all stopp?   All
com-yelow like yelow-sea?   Butt me

know nuttin mor   Cept
dey bildin tall   Dey much-like carr
much-like Wor   Dem tuch ev-where

dem stepp ev-where   Butt
me tel-me-babee – me-tink
dem ol-peepol dem juss-walk

one Gene too-farr

❧

From the next issue (summer, 95/2),
Poetry Review will be edited by Fiona Sampson.

who supports the hunger of the sky?
– Tomaz Salamun

Letters to the Editors

Grateful as I am for *Poetry Review*'s coverage of *The Faber Book of 20th-Century Italian Poems*, I'm surprised that Peter Robinson chose to review it, given that the book includes more than twenty of his own translations from twelve of the included poets. It's even more surprising that he nowhere acknowledges this fact in his review.

He must feel the disinterestedness of his motives is beyond question. Strange then that he should be so suspicious of mine, when he writes of the lack of Italian titles and sources for the poems: "That looks too like the editor covering his – as well as everyone else's – tracks." The implied accusation is groundless, and especially rich in this context. And had he read my preface as a candid statement about the book's intended scope rather than as "an all-inclusive let-out clause for any carping" at the selection, he might have saved himself his own extended fit of carping. To make the issue still clearer, I even stressed the point again in the introduction: "this book isn't . . . a fair and representative survey of Italian poetry, nor does it claim to include the best Italian poems of this period, though on both counts it doesn't score too badly." None of the suggestions he makes for inclusion would in the least prompt me to revoke the last part of that sentence.

He clearly wants the book to be an "official" anthology, equipped with a full scholarly apparatus. Faber commissioned a different kind of book (I think for good reasons) and I was happy to comply. The spirited versions by Robert Lowell, Tom Paulin and Alan Jenkins, which Robinson treats so indignantly, need no defence from me. I would have thought his own prominence in the book might have let him grant a little breathing-space to fellow-contributors, and their varied approaches to translation. That range of response to a challengingly different tradition is precisely what I hoped the book would have.

Jamie McKendrick
Oxford

I'm sorry I offended Peter Robinson's sense of propriety with my translation of Bartolo Cattafi's "Guardian Angel". I'm sure we're all better for knowing that Robinson is "on Nabokov's side" in his "old dust up with Robert Lowell" (though wasn't the dust-up actually with Edmund Wilson?); but by implication that puts me on the other side, and I'm not sure that's where I belong. Cattafi's phrase in "L'Angelo custode", describing one of the girls in a brothel, is "una italiana / dell'Italia". It establishes the speaker's taste for precision in these matters, and the girl's foreignness to him (Cataffi himself was a Sicilian). In translating it as "the eyetie piece" I went further, and tried to give the poem a voice or persona that was even more colloquial than that of the original, to accentuate something I thought I heard in it, something docks-bred, brothel-haunting. Perhaps I was wrong. I was taking a liberty, certainly. But the result isn't as "weird" as Robinson makes it sound by saying I make "the poet call one of his co-nationals something ruder than a 'limey' or 'pom'." (1) It isn't the poet, necessarily. (2) She isn't a "co-national", quite. And (3) no-one, in a brothel or anywhere else, has ever, ever referred to a woman as a "limey" or a "pom".

Alan Jenkins
London

The Poetry Society in association with Ledbury Poetry Festival
Nature Poetry in the 21st Century

A round-table discussion with poets **Deryn Rees-Jones** and **Maurice Riordan**.
Hosted by **Ruth Padel**.

Thursday 19 May at 7.30pm at **London Review Bookshop**, 14 Bury Place, London, WC1A 2JL
and **Saturday 9 July** at 12.15pm at the **Ledbury Festival**
Tickets: £6 / 4 (concessions and members)
London Box Office: 020 7420 9895 / email marketing@poetrysociety.org.uk
Ledbury Box office: 0845 458 1743 (after 8 May)

---

p o e t r y i n t r a n s l a t i o n

"Translatio, metaphora, and the leap between two worlds"
Saturday 11 June , 4.30–6.30pm at Corpus Christi College, Merton Street, Oxford OX1 4JF
A round-table discussion on the meaning of translation with poets **Carol Rumens**,
Jamie McKendrick, **Clive Wilmer** and **Oliver Taplin**. Chaired by **Ruth Padel**.
An informal wine reception and short reading by each poet will follow this.
Tickets: £5 / 4 (concessions & members) Free to Corpus Christi College students.
Box Office: 020 7420 9895 / email marketing@poetrysociety.org.uk

"Translation, Fidelity and Voice"
Sunday 17 July, 3.00–5.00pm at Dartington Festival 'Ways with Words' -
The Voice Poetry Programme
A round-table discussion with poets **Anne Born**, **Choman Hardi**, **Christopher North** and
Fiona Sampson. Chaired by Ruth Padel.
At 6pm there will be an official launch of *Poetry Review* under Fiona Sampson's editorship.
Tickets: £7 / 5.50 (concessions & members)
Box Office: 01803 867373 / email office@wayswithwords.co.uk (after 23 May 2005).
To find out more about the Way with Words Festival visit www.wayswithwords.co.uk

www.poetrysociety.org.uk

Contributors

John Ashbery's new collection, *Where Shall I Wander*, is published by Carcanet. His *Selected Prose* is reviewed on p.94.

Andrew Bailey's poems have appeared in various magazines, including *Ambit, Brittle Star, Envoi,* and *Stride*. He also sets crosswords.

Stewart Brown's most recent collection is *Elsewhere: New and Selected Poems*. He edited, with Mark McWatt, *The Oxford Book of Caribbean Verse* (2005).

Stephen Burt's second book of poetry, *Parallel Play*, will appear in February 2006; he has also edited *Randall Jarrell on W. H. Auden*, almost certainly out now. He wishes to thank David Herd and Robert Potts for years of adventure and support.

Stewart Conn lives in Edinburgh, and in 2002 was appointed to the capital's first official poet laureateship. His most recent book is *Ghosts at Cockcrow* (Bloodaxe).

William Corbett is a poet living in Boston, where he teaches at MIT and edits *Pressed Wafer*.

Andrew Duncan's most recent critical study, *Centre and Periphery in Modern British Poetry*, is published by Liverpool University Press.

Peter Gizzi's most recent collection is *Some Values of Landscape and Weather* (Wesleyan Poetry Series). This spring he received a Guggenheim Fellowship in poetry.

Brian Henry is an editor of *Verse*. His most recent book is *Graft* (Arc, 2003).

Stuart Kelly's *The Book of Lost Books* will be published by Penguin later this year.

Mimi Khalvati's *The Chine* was published by Carcanet in 2002.

Stephen Knight's book for children, *Sardines and Other Poems*, was published in 2004.

Claire Lockwood lives and works in York.

John Lyon teaches English at the University of Bristol.

Andrew McNeillie is the Literature Editor at Oxford University Press. His next book of poems, *Slower*, from which the sonnets on p.16 are taken, is due from Carcanet in July.

Lee Matthews lives in Orpington.

David Mills is a journalist who lives in London.

Sinéad Morrissey's third collection, *The State of the Prisons,* is reviewed on p.73. She is writer-in-residence at the Seamus Heaney Centre for Poetry, Belfast.

Chris Moss lived in Argentina between 1991 and 2001 and writes extensively on its literature and culture. He is currently writing *Patagonia: Landscape of the Imagination*, to be published later this year by Signal Books.

Jeremy Noel-Tod is the publisher of Landfill Press (www.landfillpress.co.uk).

Malcolm Phillips's chapbook, *Poems for My Double,* is published by Arehouse Press.

Jenni Quilter is currently completing a doctorate at Oxford University on the poetry of John Ashbery and questions of collaboration in the visual arts.

Paul Quinn is a freelance writer and programme maker.

Stephen Romer's last book of poems was *Tribute* (1998). His 20th-Century French Poems came out from Faber in 2002.

Fiona Sampson's next collection, *The Distance Between Us,* is published by Seren in May.

Simon Smith's most recent collection is *Reverdy Road* (Salt).

Julian Stannard is the author of *Rina's War* and *Fleur Adcock in Context.*

Keston Sutherland's most recent pamphlet is *Neutrality*

Fiona Wilson grew up in Aberdeen and now lives in New York. Her work appeared in *Poetry Review* 94/1 and is forthcoming in *New Writing Scotland.*

Kieron Winn's poems have appeared in *Agenda, The Rialto* and *Poetry Review.*

Jane Yeh's first full-length collection, *Marabou,* is forthcoming from Carcanet in October.